Simplified Maintenance Reliability (SMR)

How to Eliminate Downtime in Any Manufacturing Environment

Unless otherwise noted, all the content in this book, including images, text, graphics, cannot be copied or redistributed without the expressed written permission from the author.

ISBN-13: 978-1482034530

ISBN-10: 1482034530

This book is dedicated to my father Morteza Golestaneh, the greatest man I have ever known.

Acknowledgements

It took about a year to write this book, during which I struggled with many sentences and words. Meanwhile, my wife Lynette waited patiently and supported me every step of the way. For that, I am thankful to her and being there for me.

Every time I have met someone, I have learned something from him or her. After all, life is about learning good things and applying them, so others can do the same. I would like to thank my family, friends, and colleagues, from whom I have learned so much. Last but not least, I would like to thank my editor, Kristen House from Kristen Corrects.

Reader's Comments

If you have any questions or comments about this book, you can email me directly at kaveh.golestaneh@simplified-maintenance-reliability.com. I also would like to hear about your success stories after implementing the SMR program in your organization.

Contents

Introduction V

SECTION ONE 1

  Chapter One 2
    Common Maintenance Programs 2
    Obsolete Mindset 2
    Total Productive Maintenance (TPM) Shortfalls 4
    Preventative Maintenance (PM) Shortfalls 5
    Predictive Maintenance (PDM) Shortfalls 5

  Chapter Two 8
    Typical Maintenance Issues 8
    A New Paradigm 11
    Eliminating Equipment Failures 12

  Chapter Three 15
    Types of Failures 15
    Traditional Belief 19
    Age-Related Failures Categories 20
    Random Failures 21
    Normal and Abnormal Distribution 25
    Probability 26
    Normal Distribution 27
    Average (Mean) 30
    Standard Deviation 32
    Mean Time between Repairs (MBR) 36

  Chapter Four 40
    Time-Based vs. Event-Based Maintenance 40
    Event-Based Maintenance 41

Conditional or On-Condition Maintenance 41

Maintenance Options 42

PM Frequencies 45

Procedures 48

SECTION TWO 55

Chapter Five 56

Pillars of SMR 56

SMR for Manufacturing Companies 58

80/20 rule 58

4-Q Rule 59

SMR Components 60

Chapter 6 64

Severity Rankings 69

Occurrence 70

Detection 71

RPN 73

Chapter Seven 85

Implementing SMR 85

Facilitator's Role 85

Typical SMR Project 87

Action Items List 88

Hidden Failures 89

Nine Important Details to Remember 91

Chapter Eight 93

Measuring Results 93

Overall Equipment Effectiveness (OEE) 93

Estimated Replacement Value (ERV) 99

Types of Work-Orders 102
Work-Order Backlog 103
Maintenance Labor and Material Cost 105

Chapter Nine 107
Spare Parts 107
Spare Parts Strategy 108
Spare Parts Inventory Levels 110

Chapter Ten 112
New Equipment and Reliability 112
Maintenance Manuals and Service Schedules 112
Writing Specifications for Reliability 114
What is Critical? 115
Other Benefits of Simplified Maintenance Reliability 120
SMR Component Charts 126

Introduction

I have spent most my career in the metal industry and have held various positions, starting as a maintenance supervisor and working my way up to plant manager. I have held many positions in different maintenance and engineering departments, where I have always been passionate about how to make equipment more reliable. This book is the result of my thirty years of experience and research in this subject. My goal for writing this book was to introduce a scientific way of doing maintenance, and make it simple enough so everyone could understand the concept and be able to implement the program. At the end of some chapters, I have included a practice section to influence thinking and familiarize the reader with simple implementation steps.

Before we get started, I must mention a few things.

- To implement the principles in this book, you must have the support of management at all levels.
- I suggest sharing your knowledge from this book with your manager first, ensuring he or she is in support of this program, then sharing it with other managers in your company.
- This is not a quick fix, and if implemented **correctly**, the steps and programs in this book should become a way of life in your company.
- This program is not about total productive maintenance, TPM. I have implemented TPM in a few companies, and I have nothing against it. However, this program is to make your equipment more reliable, regardless of who is going to do the maintenance.

This book is divided into two sections. Section 1 familiarizes you with the types of failures, traditional belief, and maintenance options. Section 2 introduces the Simplified Maintenance Reliability (SMR) and its implementation. Make sure you understand all the principles in Section 1 before moving to Section 2.

SECTION ONE

Chapter One

Common Maintenance Programs

Most modern maintenance programs consist of some type of computerized maintenance system, several PMs for each area, annual or semiannual shutdowns, and some outsourced predictive maintenance (PDMs), normally thermography, vibration, and everyday fire fighting.

Some companies still do not have a computerized maintenance program (CMMS). The ones that do often experience that CMMS is so underutilized that it might as well not exist. Some companies have gone a step further, and developed TPM (total productive maintenance). The fact is that most of these programs have not produced the desired results. I will explain the weaknesses of these programs in some detail, so you do not follow the same incorrect road. However, before I explain the inadequacies of these programs, I am going to talk about the new technology age, and the obsolete mindset.

Obsolete Mindset

Automation keeps expanding, and there is no end in sight. This should result in better products, faster deliveries, and lesser costs.

However, the fast pace of change requires a new maintenance approach. In many cases, new technology has not produced the promised results because of the obsolete maintenance mindset.

Remember the old days? We had selector switches, relays, and linkages. Today, HMI, PLCs, and electronic probes have replaced these components. In reality, this new era has made the maintenance of the equipment much more complicated. As automation technology keeps reaching new heights, it also introduces different types of component failures that cause downtime. These failures are called random failures, and the most difficult task for any maintenance department is how to deal with these types of failures. As the name implies, we have very little knowledge of when a random failure might occur. For example, it is very difficult to detect an electronic card failure. Despite the new technology being more reliable and precise, failures occur without warnings. The traditional time-based maintenance (PMs) worked great for age-related failures such as guiderails and mechanical devices; however, it has very little success on random failures. Nevertheless, same traditional preventative maintenance is used today as it was being used decades ago: Companies have not introduced or do not know how to implement new maintenance strategies.

Companies must remove the blindfolds and develop a new strategy for asset management, and make it mandatory until it becomes a new mindset. As the market condition changes, companies quickly introduce new financial forecast and sales strategies. However, very few have developed a new program for maintaining the highly automated assets.

Failures are just like diseases: As a new disease enters our world, medical researchers immediately develop new medication to prevent, eliminate, or reduce the consequence of the disease. In the same manner, the new technology era requires an all-inclusive maintenance program that focuses on elimination, prevention, and consequence reduction of failures.

Total Productive Maintenance (TPM) Shortfalls

Many companies started implementing TPM in the 1980s. TPM is a program whose operator takes ownership of the equipment, finds failures or faults, and does minor repairs and scheduled maintenance. This program was developed at a time that companies were entering into the global economy, therefore not only it could save money on not hiring more maintenance personnel, it was presumed to be the best way of addressing the equipment failures.

However, there are two major issues with the TPM: First, the program is reactive. In other words, operator finds the failure first, then he reacts to it, and there is no prediction on when a failure might occur. Second, the maintenance issues now are being addressed by the operator that is less qualified, and in most cases, correction of more difficult and technical problems may still require qualified maintenance personnel. In most cases, the TPM programs become nothing more than machine cleanups and writing work-orders; however, the equipment failures would still exist.

In many companies, TPM has actually created higher cost—many components are replaced for no rhyme or reason, or because of the lack of knowledge of the operator, or an incorrect work performed on the equipment. Despite this, many companies that have adopted the TPM program, do not know of a better program to replace it, and therefore they keep continuing on the same path.

There is one more complication with TPM: it cannot really be implemented in some industries. In many cases, customers expect more, or regulations do not permit anyone but a highly qualified maintenance technician to perform any maintenance task. This is very true in the airline industries. Suppose you are sitting in an airport waiting to board the plane, and suddenly you hear an announcement that your plane is delayed because of a mechanical problem. You decide to go to the large glass window to see what is going on, and you observe that the same employee that was at the ticket counter ten minutes ago is now changing a hydraulic hose on the plane. How would you feel about going on the plane? Many customers demand better.

Preventative Maintenance (PM) Shortfalls

More PMs does not mean fewer failures. When I worked as a consultant in a small foundry, the molding equipment downtime was over 25 percent. The maintenance manager told me that he had written over 400 PMs for molding equipment, and he had decreased the downtime by 3 percent. My first question was why so many PMs? According to my supervisor, PMs are the answer to a good maintenance department and keeping the machine running. Obviously, you know what my answer was. This is the mindset that most managers have: more PMs, less downtime. However, this statement is far from the truth. In many cases, more PMs do not eliminate the failures. For example, having a PM for an electric motor does not prevent the motor shorting out or going to ground. Furthermore, more PMs will require more man-hours, and more man-hours equate to more maintenance people.

Predictive Maintenance (PDM) Shortfalls

Predictive maintenance is one of the better programs, as it is a proactive measurement on finding and correcting issues before they become failures and cause downtime. Vibration analysis, thermography, and oil sampling are few programs that are used in many companies today. However, there are two shortfalls with these programs: First, most of these programs are outsourced. There is no ownership of the program, and the program does not become imbedded in the culture of the company. Second, most of these programs are time-based. For example, the company performs vibration analysis on sixty motors once a month, regardless of whether monthly analysis is a proper frequency or not. Some equipment might have to be monitored once a week or once a day. Therefore, many failures still occur. I must mention an important point: *do not introduce a program just for the sake of having a program unless it can produce measurable results.*

All of the above programs are viable, but we must be aware of when and on what equipment to use them. Throughout the book I will show you how and when to use one or a combination of these programs.

Practice 1

What type of maintenance programs do you use in your company?

What is the shortfall with these programs?

1-

2-

3-

4-

5-

6-

7-

8-

9-

10-

Chapter Two

Typical Maintenance Issues

Lack of cooperation between maintenance and operations

Lack of cooperation between maintenance and operations is one of the most common problems in many companies. I am sure you have heard the excuses: "It is maintenance's fault," or "Operations broke it and blamed it on us." There are many reasons for this type of culture, but I am sure that many people would not like the answers I am going to state here.

First, I have never known of an individual with a right behavior that wanted to make a mistake intentionally. This is especially true when the mistakes happen at work. Remember this: Almost one hundred percent of all the true root causes are because of human errors. For example, if a bearing fails, it could be because of an improper design, lack of lube, or lack of inspection. Even if the bearing were made of the wrong material, it would be because someone in the manufacturing process made a mistake. Even though managers preach the same culture of teamwork and working together, there are really two different cultures existing in a company: operations and maintenance. Operations culture is the performance culture, maximizing production at the highest quality and lowest cost. Maintenance culture is the availability culture, keeping the equipment running with no downtime. Therefore, if there is a maintenance downtime, because of the definition of the root cause, there must be someone at fault, and it is hard to admit mistakes. The same holds true for operation's mistakes. In order to rectify this cultural difference, both cultures must be blended together. However, this would not happen just by preaching teamwork. Once you finish this book, you will realize how these cultures can be blended together and become one, which is the reliability culture.

High percentage of downtime

Many companies operate with 30 percent maintenance downtime, and because of the lack of success in reducing the downtime, this has become the accepted practice. Sometimes these downtimes occur after the regular PMs are completed. The fact is, however, that most maintenance PMs are incorrect for the types of failures that occur.

Equipment not running at desired or designed rate

Normally this is caused by a previous downtime that was not corrected properly or a product quality issue that was rectified by slowing down the speed. For example, a cylinder travel speed is slowed down because it would damage the product as it pushes it out of the press. As the result, cycle time of the press has increased from twenty to thirty seconds per part. This is equivalent to 33 percent production lost.

Lack of maintenance skills

Lack of maintenance skills is one of major issues in today's manufacturing environment. As the technology is becoming more advanced, many companies have not yet developed the programs to properly train employees or hire the qualified maintenance people. In 2012, there were over 300,000 job openings in technical trades such as millwrights, industrial electricians, instrument technician, and welders, and these opening will increase to 1,000,000 by 2015.

Lack of inventory of spare parts

Many companies do not stock adequate numbers or the correct spare parts. In many cases, there is no long-term program to identify what parts need to be stocked. Companies normally use the manufacturer's recommendation to determine what parts should be readily available. In many cases, when the equipment is custom made, even the manufacturer does not have the correct history or the experience to provide a correct and comprehensive list of spare parts.

Poor control of materials

A needed part has been received but cannot be located, or the part is not a correct part and it was received two years ago. I am sure everyone has gone through these types of experiences.

Inadequate or non-existent predictive, preventative, or conditional maintenance

Most likely, one of the reasons you are reading this book is to improve your maintenance program. Therefore, you must already know that you have many issues with your preventative and predictive programs. Many companies do not even have a written program to call it a maintenance program. I will discuss these issues extensively in later chapters, but for now, ask yourself: Do we have a written program that can be called the company's maintenance program? If you do not have one, start thinking about it, and ask yourself what you can do in your department. What is your philosophy, and how do you define maintenance's role in the organization? In addition, how do you rate your department? At the end of this chapter, I have a questionnaire you should fill out after you have read this book. This questionnaire will aid you in determining which areas of your maintenance department need attention.

Lack of information such as prints, manuals, procedures, work history, data, and cost

Your experience and knowledge, if applied, is invaluable; however, without the correct information, the right knowledge cannot be gained. Without the correct information, hasty decisions are made that could be costly and disastrous. Many times, companies have very little information on their major equipment, and depend on one senior individual who has worked on the equipment for many years to provide the answers. Sometimes, even the most experienced employee is puzzled by it. Therefore, many trials and errors must take place before the problem is finally solved.

Above are the typical problems in most manufacturing companies; however, the methods that I am going to share with you in this book will eliminate most of these issues.

A New Paradigm

I am going to go on record by saying: At least 70 percent of all preventative maintenance have no value, and 50 percent of the annual shutdowns are not necessary.

At this point, I might have upset some people, or they might think I am crazy. However, stay with me and let me share a story with you: Many years ago, I worked as a maintenance manager in a large company. Every year, we used to shut down the operations for two weeks to repair and overhaul the molding machines, melt furnaces, and analyze and repair the sand and pollution control systems. Six months prior to this event, planners and supervisors worked on ordering parts, scheduling work, and hiring contractors. During these shutdowns, we replaced cylinders, valves, bearings, and conveyor pans. We overhauled the molding machine. You name it, we replaced or repaired it.

The shutdowns always ended the Sunday night of the second week at 11:30 pm. The third shift operations crew would come in to start the newly repaired molding line. The maintenance crew and managers anxiously would stand by until the company made its first mold without any problems.

We were all exhausted, and wanted to go home. However, it never failed, and we always incurred many problems during the startup. Many times, these problems were extensive, and we had to shut down the operation again to replace a major part that we had just replaced few days ago. A few times, it took us two or three more weeks to get the company back in full operation mode.

I always wondered why, and never had an answer. Therefore, we always said we would do a better job next shutdown. The worst part was that every year we expected to have issues, and this had become the norm. Today I know the answer: most likely, half of the work we did during these shutdowns were not necessary. Once you understand the simplified maintenance reliability principles, you will also learn why many of these repairs are not needed, and how the shutdown length can be reduced.

Eliminating Equipment Failures

How should we eliminate equipment failures? These are some of the typical answers.

- Better preventative maintenance program
- More inspections
- Have spare parts on hand
- Implement Total Productive Maintenance
- Better operating procedures
- Train the operators
- Train the maintenance employees
- Purchase better parts

None of the previous answers can really produce a single correct response on how to eliminate equipment failures. The only answer to this question is, *in order to eliminate equipment failures, we must make the equipment one hundred percent reliable*. I did not say idiot proof—I said reliable…at least more reliable than the existing state of reliability.

The above statement is the start of our journey. Above proclamation is the only correct definition to what the maintenance role should be. Many people think the maintenance function is to keep the equipment running, and that is not the role of maintenance, because it keeps many important factors out: quality, cost, rates, etc.…

Practice 2 (Questionnaire)

Do you have written maintenance program that one can read and understand how your maintenance department conducts business?

What is your department's role in the organization?

Do you have a maintenance philosophy?

What is your vision for your department?

How do you measure the success of your maintenance department?

Is everyone in your maintenance department familiar with your philosophy?

Have you shared your vision with your department employees?

Keep all of your answers until you complete reading this book, and then you can decide whether you should use the current program or start new.

Chapter Three

Types of Failures

Faulty limit switch, worn guide rods, bearing failure, PLC card malfunction…. These examples all have their own unique types of failures. In order to make any equipment more reliable, we must first understand the types of failures and how they occur. There are four types of failures.

1. Age-associated gradual (or slow)
2. Age-associated immediate (or sudden)
3. Random Gradual
4. Random immediate (or sudden)

Age-Associated Failures

Failure that occurs when a component has reached its useful life under normal operating conditions is called an age-associated failure.

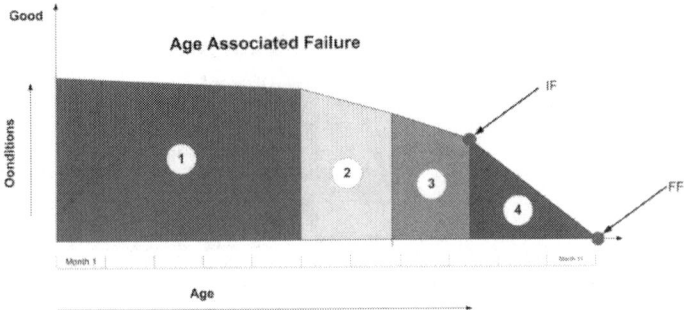

Figure 3.1. Age-associated failures

Figure 3.1 demonstrates this type of failure. At the beginning, the component is running in good condition for many months, years, or cycles. However, at some point, it starts showing some wear or lack of performance, which might not be noticeable at first. Area 2 represents this condition. Then, the component will reach a state that the lack of performance is more noticeable; however, it is still performing within the desired limits. Area 3 represents this condition. Finally, the component does not function properly and causes hindrance to the operation. The starting point of this condition is the initial failure point, IF. At this point, if the problem is not corrected, the component will reach its final failure point, FF.

Types of Age-Associated Failures

There are two types of age-associated failures: Gradual and Immediate. Immediate failures are also known as sudden failures.

Age-associated gradual failures are age-related failures that happen slowly; they are detectible.

An example of this type of failure would be the tires on your car. During their life, you might get a few flat tires; however, under normal conditions, tires should operate properly for 50,000 miles before you might notice tread loss or lack of traction. At this point, you should replace them. You can notice the initial failure with proper inspection. For instance, tires can be inspected visually with a tire tread gauge, and initial failure can be detected. Figure 3.2 shows a typical age-associated gradual failure. Please note that there is a time span, T, between the initial Failure IF, and the final failure, FF.

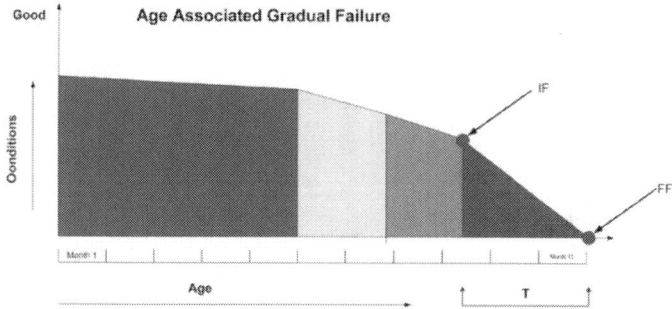

Figure 3.2. Age-associated gradual failure

Age-associated sudden failures are age-related failures in which there is no time between the initial failure and the final failure, and happens without prior indication.

An example would be an electric motor. The electric motor may operate properly for many years, and suddenly it does not start. There was no prior warning of imminent failure.

Figure 3.3 shows typical age-related sudden failures. On the left figure, the component might lose performance; however, this might not be noticeable, and then the component would suddenly fail. On the right figure, the component will operate properly for ten months with absolutely no signs of wear or lack of performance, and then it suddenly stops working. Normally, these types of components have a known life expectancy, and the failures are predictable. Think of how many components you can name in your plant that last about a year, and then you have to replace them.

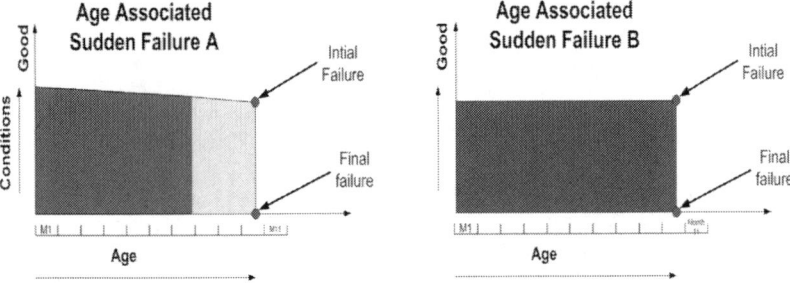

Figure 3.3. Age-associated sudden failures

Examples of Age-Associated Failures

These are some the examples of components with age-related gradual failures.

- Slides
- Engines
- Compressors
- Chutes
- Liners
- Vessels
- Linkages
- Hydraulic or air cylinders
- Gear Boxes

In addition, these are some of the examples of components with age-related immediate or sudden failures:

- Mechanical relays
- Mechanical limit switches
- Electric motors
- Mechanical starters
- Vacuum pumps
- Push buttons or selector switches

Traditional Belief

For many decades, there has been a belief that all failures are age-related. In other words, every piece of equipment has a useful life, and when the end of this life has been reached, the equipment must be overhauled or replaced. This belief still exists today in most industries. This is called the bathtub curve. Figure 3.4 represents this belief.

The bathtub curve indicates that at the beginning of the equipment's life, the equipment has a high chance of failure, likely due to start-up issues. Following its initial phase, the equipment has equal chances of failure for a period of time, and once the equipment reaches its useful life, the chances of failures increase again. At this point, the machinery needs either to be replaced or overhauled. One example of the traditional belief would be reciprocating air compressors.

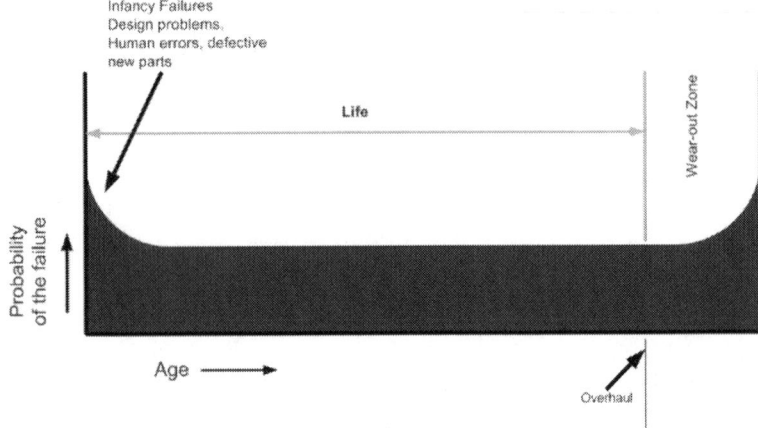

Figure 3.4. Bathtub curve

At the beginning of its life, the air compressor might have several issues. These could be in form of startup problems, human errors, and faulty components. Once these problems are resolved, the air compressor operates with few failures. These failures have equal chances of occurring. The air compressor operates this way for many years, and at some point, the failures start increasing. Once this occurs, the air compressor must be overhauled or replaced.

Age-Related Failures Categories

Figure 3.5 represents the categories of the age-associated failures. There are three categories of age-associated failures. Category 1 is the bathtub curve, this type of failure accounts for 4 percent of total failures. Category 2 is similar to the bathtub curve; however, the chances of infancy failures do not increase. Your car engine is a perfect example for this category. Only 2 percent of total failures fall in this category. Finally, the third category is linear. Chances of failures linearly increase as the equipment becomes older. Examples for this category would be guides, bushings, and rails. These types of failures account for 5 percent of total failures. Therefore, Only 11 percent of failures are age-related. So, what are the other 89 percent of the failures?

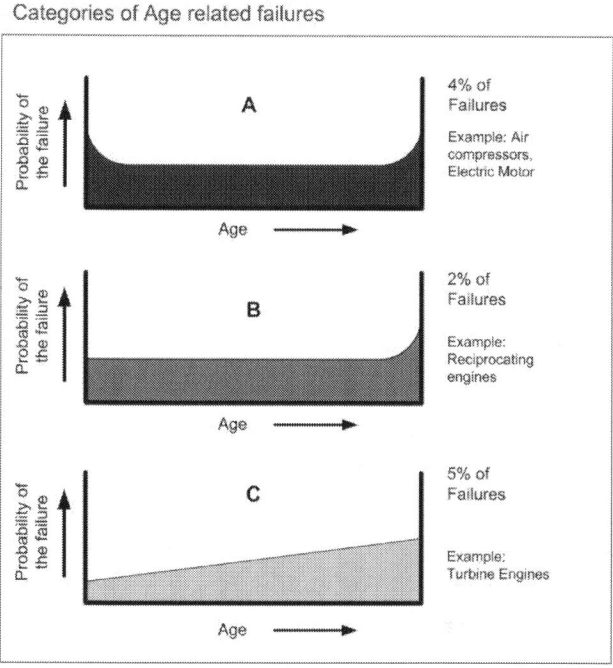

Figure 3.5. Age-related failure categories

Random Failures

Random failures are defined as equal chances of failure with having no specific pattern. The light bulb is a good example: it might be rated for eight hundred hours of average life, but it might last one hour, or a thousand hours. You never know when a light bulb is going to fail.

Random failures account for 89 percent of all failures. The most difficult task for the maintenance department is how to deal with these types of failures. Overhaul and replacement produces little results, and inspections do not amount to much success. As I mentioned before, there are two types of random failures: random gradual (or slow) failures; or random immediate (or sudden).

Random Gradual Failures

Random gradual failures are failures in which there is a time span between the initial failure (IF) and the final failure (FF). It is important to note that random gradual failures can be detected because of this time span. These failures show some sign of initial failure mode. Figure 3.6 shows a typical random gradual failure.

Please look at Figure 3.6. Since this is a random failure, initial failure can happen at any time. IF1, 2, 3, and 4 represent these initial failures. FF1, 2, 3, and 4 are the corresponding final failure points when the component no longer functions. Now notice the time span between each IF and FF: T1 is the time span between the initial failure one (IF1) and final failure one (FF1). This time span could be ten minutes or one year, and would depend on the component. However, if the initial failure is detected, we can develop a maintenance program to prevent the final failure. This will be explained in Section 2.

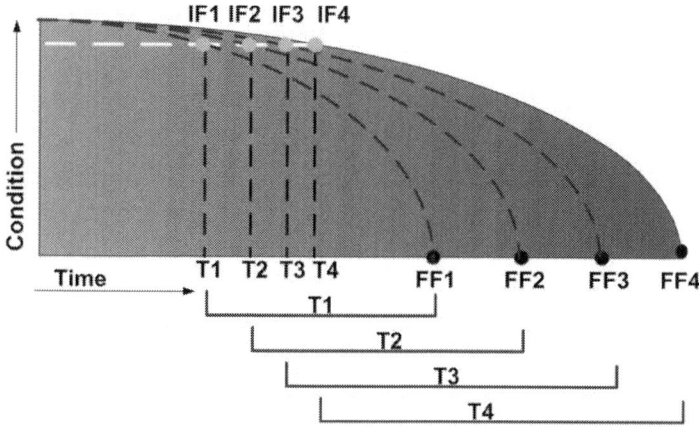

Figure 3.6. Random gradual failures

Random Immediate Failures

Random immediate or sudden failures are random failures where there is no time span between the initial failure (IF) and the final failure (FF). The best examples of these failures are PLC cards or proximity switches. Please look at Figure 3.7. As it is obvious, unlike the random gradual failures, there is no time between IF and FF. These types of failures are the hardest failures to prevent, as it is almost impossible to detect and prevent a PLC card failure. Later, in Section 2, I will discuss our options to deal with these types of failures.

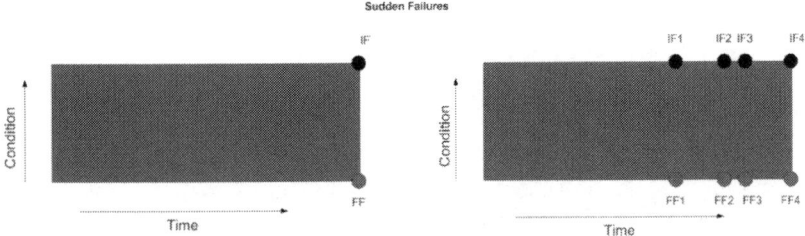

Figure 3.7. Random sudden failures

As aforementioned, fifty percent of annual shutdowns are not necessary. Here is the reason: Not every failure is an age-associated failure. If we want to improve the reliability of the equipment, we must erase in our mind that all equipment has a useful life expectancy. In most manufacturing companies, it is the belief that all equipment follows the bathtub curve, and that is simply not the truth. For many manufacturing companies, overhauling and replacing the equipment is not the answer to reliability.

Examples of Random Failures

- DC power supplies
- Electrical switches such as proximity, read switch, and magnet switches
- Computers
- Programmable controller cards
- Transducers
- Light bulbs
- Instrumentations

- Coils
- Inductors
- Capacitors
- Hydraulic valves
- Air logic components
- Pneumatic components
- Thermo-couples
- RF transducers
- Relays
- Starters
- DC and AC variable speed controllers

These were just a few examples. I am sure you can find many more components in your plant subject to random failures.

Normal and Abnormal Distribution

It is not my intention to use complex formulas and to complicate the chapter; however, it is important to understand the concepts of normal and abnormal distribution. You do not need to memorize the formulas, as many of these formulas are available in spreadsheet programs if needed. Do not spend time on understanding formulas, but make sure you understand the concepts.

Probability

Probability means chances. What are the chances of getting a flat tire while driving from your house to work? A fair dice has six equal sides; therefore, when throwing a dice, the probability of getting a 1 through 6 is 1/6 or 16.67 percent. In this example, the probability of getting a 1 through 6 is equal because the dice is fair. However, if the dice was loaded, we might get more sixes than the rest of the numbers. Also, one must remember if the dice is thrown only a few times—for example, ten times—we might get a 1 six times, a 4 three times, and a 5 one time. However, in the long term, the more the dice is thrown, the actual number of getting a 1 through 6 would be much closer to the probability of 16.67 percent. In other words, in the short term, anything could happen; however, in the long term, the actual numbers will reach the calculated probability.

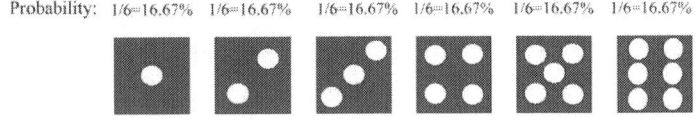

Figure: 3.8. Probability of dice.

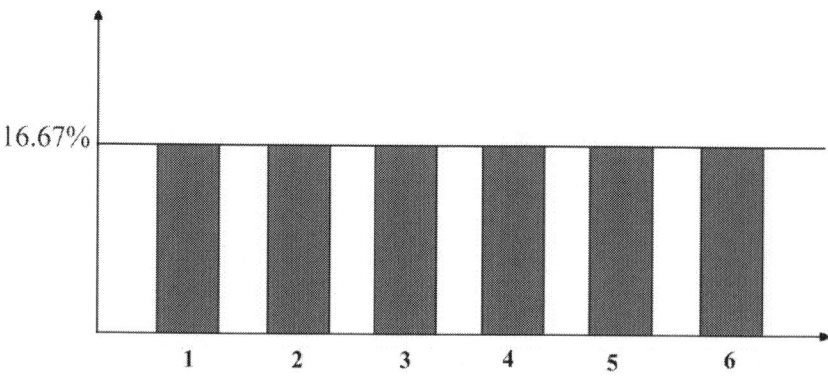

Figure: 3.9. Equal chances of getting a 1 through 6.

Normal Distribution

Let's look at throwing two dices together at the same time. Figure 3.10 shows the probability of throwing two fair dices. As the figure illustrates, there are thirty-six possible ways of getting a 2 through 12. For example, there are only two ways to get a three: if the first dice is a 2 and the second dice is a 1, or if the first dice is a 1 and the second dice is a 2. There are no other ways to get a 3; therefore, the probability of getting a 3 is two out of thirty-six, or 5.56 percent. Figure 3.11 illustrates the probability of all the possible outcomes of two dices thrown. What is important to understand: unlike the single dice, probabilities of the outcome are not equal. However, as long as we are using a pair of fair dice, the outcomes are predictable.

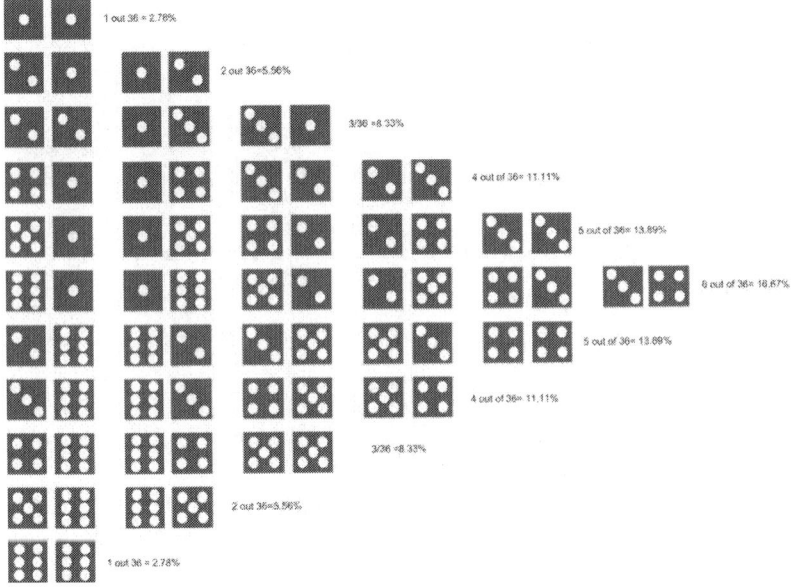

Figure: 3.10. Possible outcome of a pair of dice

Outcome		Probability
2	1 out of 36	2.78%
3	2 out of 36	5.56%
4	3 out of 36	8.33%
5	4 out of 36	11.11%
6	5 out of 36	13.89%
7	6 out of 36	16.67%
8	5 out of 36	13.89%
9	4 out of 36	11.11%
10	3 out of 36	8.33%
11	2 out of 36	5.56%
12	1 out of 36	2.78%

Figure 3.11. Pair of dice outcome table

If dices were thrown only a few times—for example, ten times—the outcome would not match Figure 3.11. However, if the dices were thrown on a long term basis—for example, a thousand times—the outcome would start matching the table. Figure 3.12 shows the distribution of pair of a dice. This is called a normal distribution. As long as the dices are fair, the outcome would be the same as Figure 3.12.

Normal distribution always has a shape of a bell. The reason for the shape of the normal distribution is that the chances of getting a 2 through 12 are inherent to the configuration and the shape of the dice. Therefore, chance causes or system causes are causes that are built in the process and are always present in the process. In addition, a process with chance causes alone tends to vary in a normal and predictable manner.

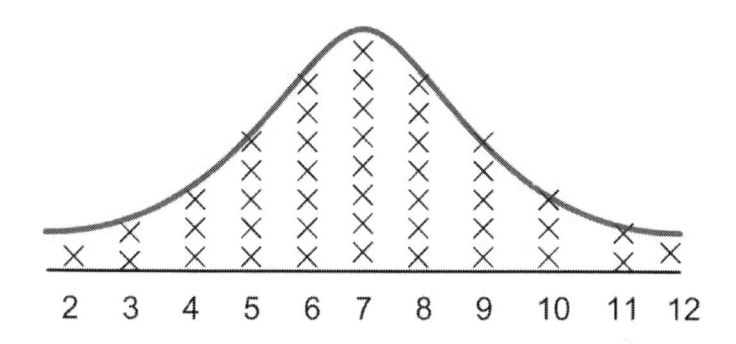

Figure 3.12. Normal distribution of a pair of dice

Let's assume that dices were loaded and not fair. Figure 3.13 shows the distribution of the loaded pair of dice. Once the dices are loaded, the distribution will lose its normal bell shape. For example, Figure 3.13a shows that we would seldom get a twelve.

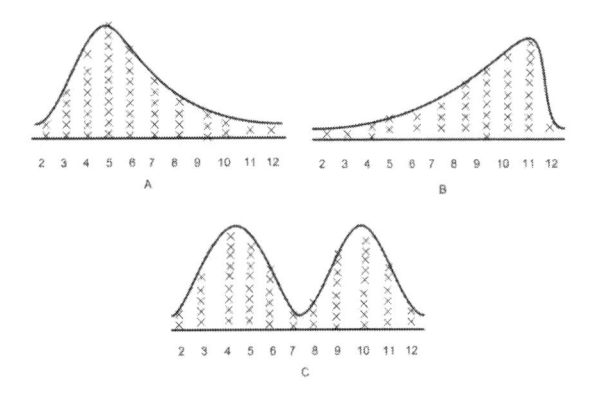

Figure 3.13. A, B, C: Abnormal distribution

Therefore, assigned causes, or special causes, are defined as causes that are not always active in the process; instead, they are causes that we are able to correct. For example, loading a pair of dice is a special cause. The pit boss would quickly replace the pair of dice with a new pair. Here, we used the dice example, but special causes could be in the form of downtime, equipment not operating properly, or operational issues.

Average (Mean)

Joe has been bowling for three years and has kept all of his scores; however, he does not know his average score. One day he decides to calculate this average, but he has over two hundred numbers, which makes the task complicated. He decides to put all the numbers in a bag and pick thirty of them at random. Table 3.1 shows Joe's scores sample.

1	156		17	190
2	175		18	200
3	174		19	205
4	177		20	177
5	210		21	185
6	180		22	225
7	197		23	225
8	165		24	175
9	197		25	156
10	175		26	160
11	173		27	205
12	200		28	200
13	208		29	205
14	275		30	188
15	300			5843
16	185	Average		194.7667 ≈ 195

Table 3.1. Joe's random sampling

Joe's bowling average from the sample is approximately 195, which is simply the sum of the bowling scores (5843) divided by the number of samples, which is 30. This is called the sample population mean. At this point, Joe knows that 50 percent of the scores are over 195, and the other 50 percent are less than 195. Figure 3.14 represents the population of Joe's scores.

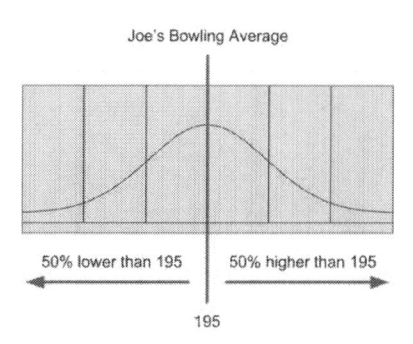

Figure 3.14. Bowling scores mean

Standard Deviation

It is important to understand the concept of standard deviation, because it becomes important in making many decisions. Standard deviation is a mathematical calculation of the amount of variation or spread in a process data, and it is represented by the following formula.

$$s = \sqrt{\frac{1}{N-1}\sum_{i=1}^{N}(x_i - \overline{x})^2}$$

Where N is the number of samples, X is the each data in the sample and $\overline{x}$ is the mean.

Figure 3.15 shows the properties of a normal distribution and standard deviation.

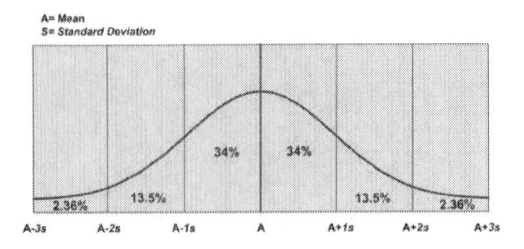

Figure 3.15. Normal distribution properties

Following are the properties of the normal distribution:

- 34 percent of the data falls between the mean, and mean plus one standard deviation.
- 13.5 percent of data falls between the A+1S, and A+2s.
- 2.36 percent of data falls between A+2s, and A+3s.
- 34 percent of the data falls between the mean, and mean minus a one standard deviation.

- 13.5 percent of data falls between A-1s and A-2s.
- 2.36 percent of data falls between A-2s and A-3s

In the case of Joe's scores sample, I used a common spreadsheet program to calculate the standard deviation, and it turned out to be 30. Figure 3.16 shows the distribution of Joe's scores.

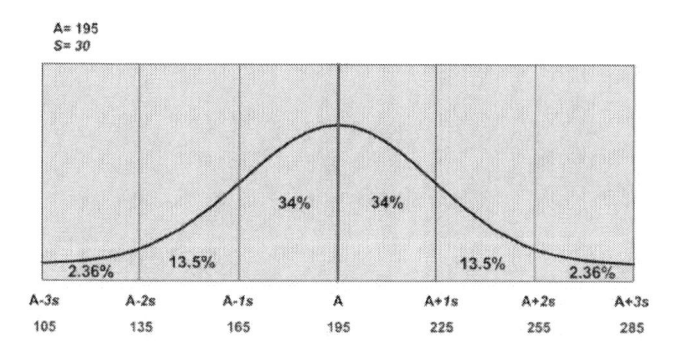

Figure 3.16. Joe's standard deviation for the bowling scores

Now Joe can easily realize his score spread. For example, 34 percent of the time, Joe's bowling score is between 195 and 225. At 2.36 percent of the time, he bowls between 255 and 285. You might wonder why I had to talk about normal distribution and standard deviation, and what these concepts have to do with maintenance of equipment—it has everything to do with equipment downtime! Let's assume instead of Joe's bowling scores, this data represented the days that the guide rods on a high-speed press operated before failure (Table 3.2 and figure 3.17). Remember, we are using the same data as Joe's scores.

Press Guide Rod Failure History (Days)

1	156	17	190
2	175	18	200
3	174	19	205
4	177	20	177
5	210	21	185
6	180	22	225
7	197	23	225
8	165	24	175
9	197	25	156
10	175	26	160
11	173	27	205
12	200	28	200
13	208	29	205
14	275	30	188
15	300		5843
16	105	Average	194.7667 ≈ 195

Table 3.2. Sample data for the press guide

Press Guide Rod Failure, Normal Distribution

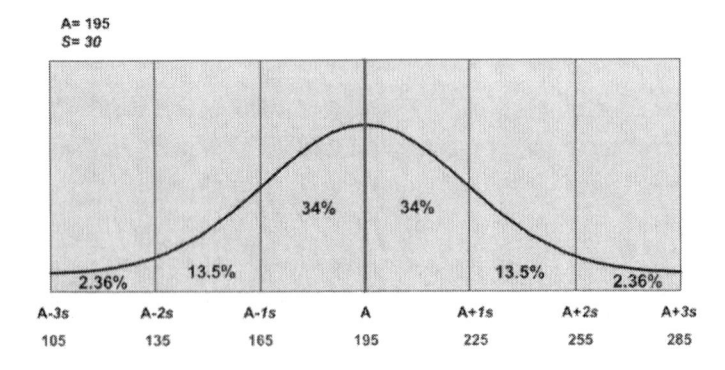

A= 195
S= 30

A-3s	A-2s	A-1s	A	A+1s	A+2s	A+3s
105	135	165	195	225	255	285

2.36% | 13.5% | 34% | 34% | 13.5% | 2.36%

Figure 3.17. Press guide normal distribution

A few important facts from Figure 3.17 become obvious.

- 195 days is the mean time between the failures (MBF). Mean time between failures is the sum of days that guide rod operated before failure (TBF) divided by number of failures, N.

$$MBF = \frac{(T1+T2+T3+\ldots Tn)}{N}$$

- 50 percent of failures happen before 195 days. In other words, if we had a replacement program at 195 days, 50 percent of the failures would still occur.
- The failure rate between 135 days and 105 days is 2.36 percent.
- 99.72 percent of failures would happen before the guide rods reach 285 days, which is the total of 2.36 percent + 13.5 percent + 34 percent + 34 percent + 13.5 percent + 2.36 percent.

To minimize the failure, we know that the replacement schedule should be before the 195 days, because we know that 50 percent of failures happen on or before this point. The question remains: When should we replace the guide rods? The answer to this question might seem easy. On first thought, we might say they should be replaced before 105 days. However, there are many factors play in the right decision.

- How much risk the company is willing to take?
- What is the cost of the replacement?
- What is the cost of downtime, and loss of sales or a quality issue that might rise from the failure?
- What is the impact to the bottom line?

Mean Time between Repairs (MBR)

Let us assume that in the last example, we are going to replace the guides between 105 and 135 days. In other words, we are not willing to take more than 2.36 percent chances of failure. Table 3.3 shows the ten replacements that have been between 105 and 135 days.

$$MTR = \frac{(TR1+TR2+TR3+... TRnr)}{NR}$$

TR= Mean time between repair

NR= Number of repairs

Repair	Days
1	110
2	111
3	110
4	111
5	120
6	120
7	124
8	117
9	116
10	115
Total	1154
Average	115

Table 3.3. Press guide replacement data

From Table 3.3, the average between replacements is 115 days. This is called the mean time between repairs. Mean time between repairs (MBR) is the sum of the total days between repairs divided by the number of repairs. I have used a spreadsheet program to calculate the standard deviation for the repairs data in Table3.3, and it is five days. Therefore, the normal distribution would look like Figure 3.18.

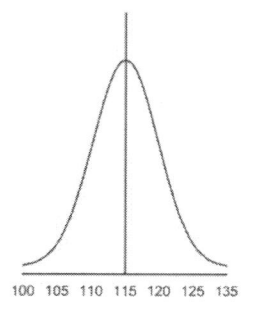

Figure 3.18. Standard distribution between repairs

In reality, for the above example, it is not important to calculate the standard deviation for the mean time between repairs. However, we need to know that in order to keep the chances of failure to 2.36 percent, our repairs need to be between 105 to 135 days or less.

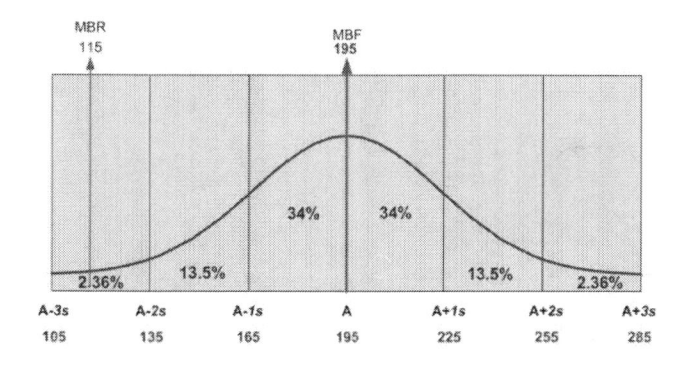

Figure 3.19. MBF and MBR of the press guides

Different PMs for Different Times

Once again, I am going to use an example to illustrate an important point that is missed in many companies, which causes many wasted maintenance man-hours and productivity. Let's assume that we have a monthly PM program for the guiderails in Figure 3.23A. I have purposely chosen monthly PMs to be the same as standard deviation to make the illustration easier. Figure 3.20b shows the mean time between the failures and the day zero, when the guiderail has been replaced. The next PM is due in one month. There are approximately 9 PMs before we reach a point that there is a 2.36 percent chance of failure.

Since the PM intervals are every thirty days, and equal to the standard deviation, the first PM is eleven standard deviations away from the mean. Therefore, at the first PM, the chance of failure is almost zero. As we move from the first PM to the ninth PM, chances of failure start increasing, but they are still minimal.

Thus, if the chance of failure at PM 1 is near zero, should the PM 1 be the same as the PM 6, or the PM 9? Most companies have the same PM for the PM 1 through PM 9. This is because no one has paid any attention to when the failure starts to happen. Now suppose this PM took a man two hours to perform, but operation had to stop for the duration of the PM. For 9 PMs, there would be eighteen maintenance man-hours, and operation lost that cannot be recovered.

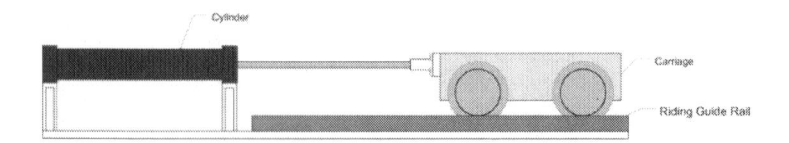

Figure 3.20a. Moving carriage

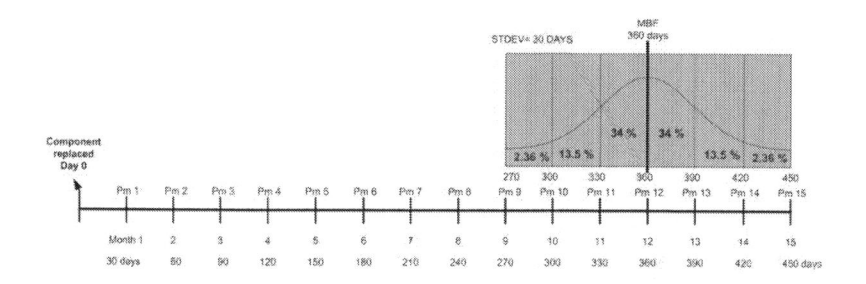

Figure 3.20b. Mean time between failures and the PM schedule

In reality, the PMs 1, 2, 3, 4, 5, and 6 should be quick visual checks, making sure that the rails are tight and not worn. PMs 7, 8, and 9 should be some type of wear measurement and/or NDT for cracks. In other words, as we get closer to the MBF, we should perform meaningful PMs more often, and we should not waste much time on the PMs that are so distant from the mean that the failures are highly unlikely to happen.

Remember that what I have discussed here only applies to age-associated failures, and not random failures. I am not suggesting eliminating all of the initial PMs; however, I am implying that you should review the PMs and make them more efficient. In the life span of any component, the same component would require different PMs at different times.

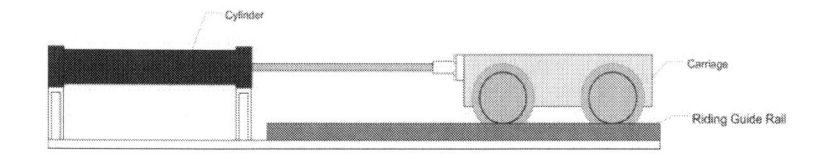

Figure 4.1. Moving carriage

Chapter Four

Time-Based vs. Event-Based Maintenance

Most companies use time-based maintenance as their primary method of discovering the initial failures and addressing issues. Time-based maintenance is defined as maintenance inspections or repairs that are performed based on a time schedule; for example, once a week, once a month, or once a year.

Time-based maintenance is very effective for age-associated gradual failures. However, it is not effective with random and age-related sudden failures. For example, there is no time-based inspection that can detect a motor going to ground or shorting out.

Figure 4.1 represents a carriage that moves forward and back on the riding rails. Let us assume that the system is designed in such a way that the connection between the cylinder and the carriage can handle one eighth of an inch downward movement. However, any more movement could damage the cylinder and the coupling. In addition, the system is designed that the surfaces of the wheels are of softer material than the rails. In other words, wheels are wearable items by design.

Time-based maintenance could work well for the above example—for instance, checking the diameter of the wheels once a week and comparing it with the design specification. If the wheels are worn more than the desired limits, they will be replaced.

Event-Based Maintenance

Event-based maintenance is defined as repairs or replacement of a component or components based on an event or an indication prior to the final failure.

We can implement an event-based maintenance for the last example. We would install a distance-measuring device on the moving part of the carriage. This device continuously measures the distance between the carriage and the rail. If the distance decreases by a tenth of an inch, the alarm would sound, and it is time to change the wheels. The alarm would be the event. Setting the limit lower allows us to plan the replacement of the wheels.

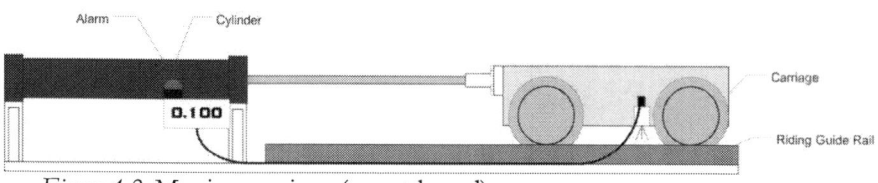

Figure 4.2. Moving carriage (event-based)

Conditional or On-Condition Maintenance

Conditional maintenance, also known as on-condition maintenance, is a type of an event-based maintenance and defined as continuously checking for the initial failure, so that action can be taken to prevent the failure or to avoid the consequence of that failure. By checking, I imply trending, testing, statistical determination, and monitoring the equipment.

The last example represents a conditional maintenance, because the conditions of the wheels are being continuously monitored.

The following list shows some of the conditional maintenance monitoring.

- Vibration
- Temperature
- Air flow
- Distance
- Liquid flow
- Pressure
- Level
- Ultrasound
- Contamination check
- Power
- Calibration Check
- Power Factor and x-ray

Maintenance Options

Most people believe that a proper equipment inspection or PMs will correct all equipment issues, and maintenance has many options to prevent failures. This is far from the truth. As you have learned, not every failure can be detected. The reality is that there are only a few options available, and what option to use depends on the type of failure. However, if the correct option is used, it can eliminate or at least drastically reduce the chance of failures. Let's review these maintenance options.

There are four maintenance options for age-associated slow failures:

1. Time-based maintenance (TM)
2. Time-based replacement (TR)
3. Event-based maintenance (EB)
4. Training (T)

There are four maintenance options for age-associated sudden failures.

1. Time-based replacement (TR)
2. Redundant systems (Redundancy)
3. Frequent variation monitoring (VM)
4. Training (T)

I will explain the variation monitoring later in an example.

There are four maintenance options for random slow failures.

1. Event-based maintenance (EB)
2. Redundant systems (Redundancy)
3. Training (T)
4. Frequent variation monitoring (VM)

There are five maintenance options for random sudden failures.

1. Run to failure (RF)
2. Redundant systems (Redundancy)
3. Reengineering alternatives (RA)
4. Frequent variation monitoring (VM)
5. Training (T)

Maintenance Option Chart

Table 4.1 shows the maintenance option chart. This chart is very important, and will be used extensively once you implement SMR program in your plant.

	Sudden (S)	Gradual (G)
Age- associated (A)	Time Based Replacement. (TR) Redundant Systems. Frequent Variation Monitoring. (VM) Training. (T)	Time Based Maintenance. (TM) Time Based Replacement. (TR) Event Based Maintenance. (EB) Training. (T)
Random (R)	Run to Failure. (RF) Redundant Systems. Reengineering Alternatives. (RA) Frequent Variation Monitoring. (VM). Training.(T).	Event Based Maintenance. (EB) Redundant Systems. Training. (T). Frequent Variation Monitoring. (VM)

Table 4.1. Maintenance operation chart

On the right column, you will notice age-associated failure designated by letter (A), and random failure designated by letter (R). Also on the top row, you will notice sudden failure, which is designated by letter(s), and gradual failure designated by letter (G). Therefore, if a failure is a random sudden, the designation would be (RS). In the same manner, if the failure is an age-related gradual, the designation would be AG.

The rest of the chart shows the maintenance options available for each type of failure. For example, if the failure is random gradual (RG), the corresponding maintenance options are event-based maintenance, redundant systems, frequent variation monitoring, and training. Once you start using the maintenance option chart on a regular basis, all the acronyms become easily memorized.

PM Frequencies

I am going to discuss an important subject that costs many maintenance hours, and it goes without notice in many manufacturing companies. Figure 4.3 shows an example of an age-related gradual failure. This could be rollers, guides, or a pump. Let's assume that we have developed an annual PM, which is the same thing as a time-based maintenance. The first blue line indicates this PM timeline.

However, the final failure happens before the inspection is due. By right, the manager of the department is very upset, and he or she makes it clear that our maintenance program is not working because our plant incurred two hours of downtime. Therefore, we decide to increase the PM frequency to a semiannual PM, and we assure the manager that we would address this problem, and we would catch it next time.

Therefore, we perform the first PM on time and we find no issues with the equipment. However before the next PM is due, failure happens again. Please look at the second blue line that shows the semiannual inspection timeline. At this point, the manager is very unhappy, discouraged, and has lost faith in our ability to maintain his or her equipment. Therefore, we decide to increase the PM frequency again. This time we increase the frequency to quarterly inspections. In the first, second, and the third PM, we would find the equipment healthy and with no issues. However, before the fourth PM is due, the failure happens again. At this point, the manager is furious and does not understand why we cannot get it right and catch this failure. Therefore, manager tells us that he or she wants this piece of equipment checked monthly. At this point, we would increase our PM to a monthly inspection. Notice the bottom blue line that represents the monthly PM. After performing nine inspections, we finally catch the problem and correct it. Now the manager is very happy and buys everybody a lunch, and tells us: "That's how we can solve the problem: by increasing the frequency of the inspections, and this is the answer to a successful maintenance department." What went wrong in this example?

Suppose the equipment was a pump that took two hours to replace. Think about this example. This has happened in every company I have worked at, and I am sure it is happening in yours too.

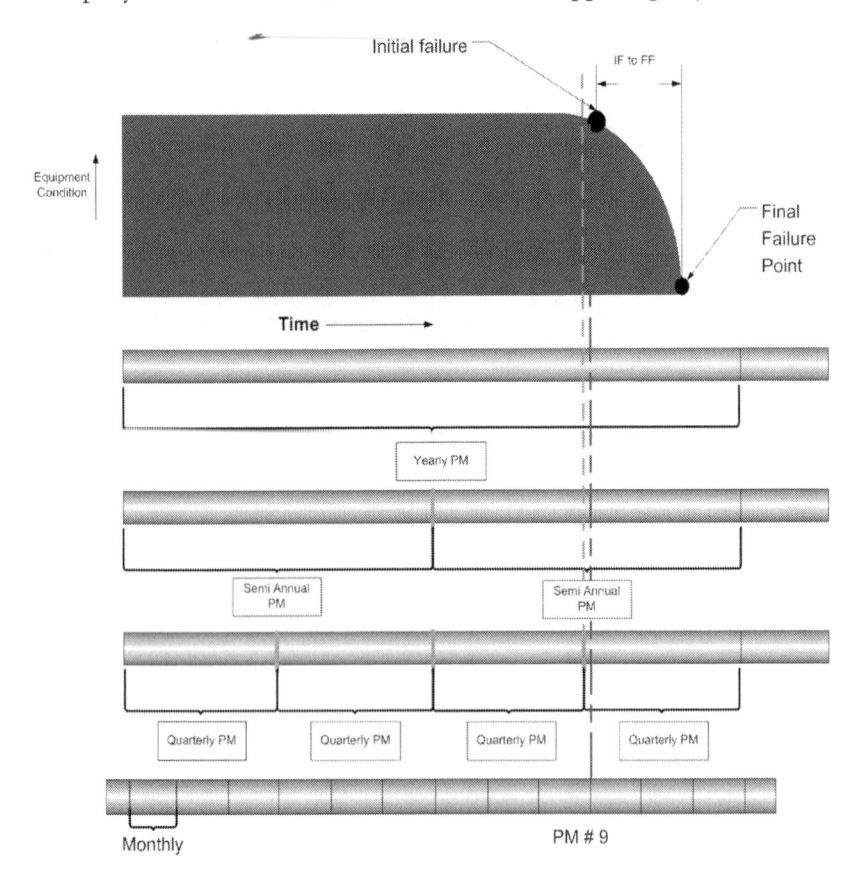

Figure 4.3. PM frequency

What Went Wrong?

First, let's look at the hours spent on this equipment to detect the initial failure. Let's assume it took four hours to inspect the equipment each time.

At first, for the annual inspection, we spent four hours. When we chose to increase our frequency to semi-annual inspection, we used eight hours. For the quarterly inspection, we spent sixteen hours, and when we increased our PM to monthly inspections, we increased our maintenance hours to thirty-six. It is important to note that some of the frequency increases did not help us to discover the issue. In reality, we spent thirty-two more man-hours on this piece of equipment, which means more man-hours are lost in attempt to prevent failure than if the failure had actually happened. I do not know what the hourly rates with benefits are for the maintenance employees in your company; however, the cost could be significant.

One might say the end justifies the means. However, suppose you have a hundred examples like this, and you had to increase the PM frequency for each one. That would be about 3200 man-hours, which equates to approximately two more employees.

Next, suppose it took four hours to replace the pump. Why would you put four hours to PM the pump, and furthermore, why would you increase the PM frequency, and spend thirty-six hours on it?

So what is the answer? Simply, the maintenance option that was used is incorrect. As I mentioned at the beginning of this example, this was an age-related gradual failure. All age-related gradual failures are predictable. As you saw in the last slide, this piece of equipment operated properly for nine months before the initial failure. Therefore, the proper maintenance method would be time-based replacement, or an event-based maintenance. For the time-based maintenance, we would change the pump every six to seven months. For event-based maintenance, we would install some type of monitoring system to monitor the condition of the equipment continuously. This could be in form of vibration or temperature monitoring or a system that appropriate for the application.

I am not saying we should install some kind of monitoring system on every piece of equipment or replace every piece of equipment every so often—I am simply saying that we should choose the correct maintenance option for each one.

Let me tell you a funny story: I worked in a company in a town where the drinking water did not taste right. Therefore, all of the drinking fountains—approximately fifty of them—had water filtrations. Part of our quarterly maintenance PM was to replace the water filters. The cost of the filter was sixty dollars, and it took us about a half hour to replace each one. However, since it was not on our priority list, they were hardly replaced on time, until somebody complained. It did not take us long to figure out that it was cheaper and much easier to buy purified water than to replace filters.

Sometimes it is justified to spend thirty-six man-hours to inspect something that takes four hours to replace. There are cases when there are no other options because of the location or the type of the equipment. Also in some cases, there is no monitoring system available to determine the condition of the equipment.

This brings us to a subject called secondary failures. The secondary failure is the resultant failure of the primary failure. For example, if a pump fails, it might take a couple of hours to replace, and by itself, it might not be significant. However, if this pump was producing water to a coil in an induction furnace, the secondary failure could be the damage to the coil, which might cause a run out, which could shutdown the operation, which could delay the deliveries, or cause injuries. Sometimes, the secondary failures are much more significant than the primary failures. In cases when secondary failures are significant and there are no monitoring or replacement methods available, the frequent inspections are justified if and only if they can detect the failure or prevent the consequences of that failure. However, today with the computer age, anything can be monitored. It just depends on the application.

Procedures

Sometimes, procedures that are created to improve the processes create major problems, because they give us false sense of security.

For example, let's look at an iron transfer crane with a weight scale. Suppose we have written a quality procedure that states the scale needs to be calibrated every four weeks. In addition, a calibration sticker must be put on the scale in a visible area. Procedure also states that the scale should not be calibrated any sooner than one week before the due date.

In Figure 4.4, the striped lines represent the timeline, and the vertical arrow is the time that we performed the calibration. The next calibration is not due for another four weeks. One week later, on second shift, the crane operator accidentally runs the crane into the end stops of the rails. This throws the scale out of calibration. However, no damage is done to the crane. At this point, the operator has no way of knowing if the scale is out of tolerance, and continues running the crane for the next transfer. Since the next calibration is not due for three weeks, the crane could operate incorrectly and the wrong amount of alloys could be added to the ladle. This could go unnoticed, because the sticker states that the scale was just calibrated recently.

Now, please understand I am not saying procedures are bad. Actually, I am in favor of operating procedures. However, before any procedure is developed, we must understand the type of the failure and its maintenance options.

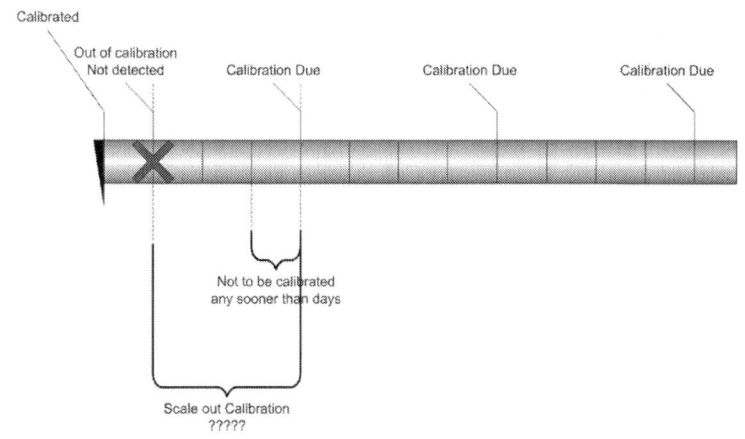

Figure 4.4. Scale calibration

In the above example, the failure is a random sudden, time-based maintenance—in this case, monthly calibration does not prevent this failure. In fact, there are no methods available to prevent this type of failure. However, we can prevent the consequence of it.

The approach should be variation monitoring. The operator should check the scale with a known weight, maybe once per shift or once per day. The frequency depends on the company's preference, and what risk the company can accept. In addition, the results should be documented, and if there is a discrepancy between the scale and the known weight, the scale should immediately be calibrated or repaired. This would minimize the consequence of the failure.

It is important to remember this statement again: Before any procedure is developed, we must understand the type of the failure and its maintenance options to prevent that failure or the consequence of that failure.

Exercise One

I will go through this exercise with you. Figure 4.5 shows a blower, and I have identified seven major components: motor, motor mounts, belts, main bearings, sheaves, shaft, and the fan impeller.

In the Exercise 1, we are going to identify potential and the type of failure for each component.

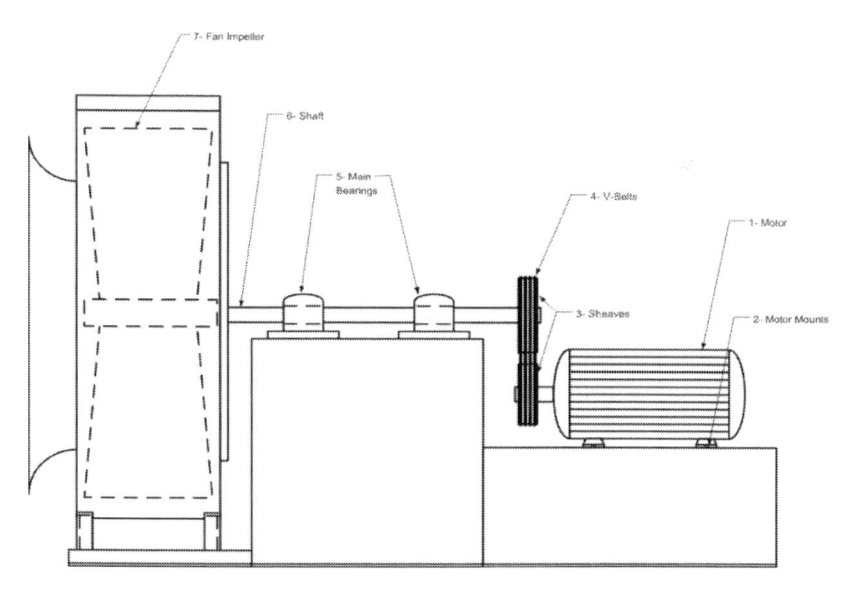

Figure 4.5. Exercise 1, blower component

Line	Component and Function	Potential Failure Mode	Type of Failure
1	Motor	Motor grounded/ shorted	AS
2		Bearing failure	RG
3		Lack or over Lube of bearing	RG
4	Motor mounts	One come loose	AG
5	Sheaves	Wear	AG
6		Hub breaking	AS
7	Belts	Belt break	AG
8		Belt break	AS
9	Main bearings	Bearings failing	RG
10		Bearings Failure	RG
11		Bearings Failure	RG
12	Shaft	Shaft failing	RS
13		Shaft failing	RG/ RS
14	Fan impeller	Impeller worn	AG
15		Imbalance	AS

Table 4.2. Types of failures for blower component

Please look at Table 4.2. The first component is the motor, and I have identified three failures for this component. The first failure could be the motor grounded, or shorted. This is an age-associated sudden failure, AS. The second failure is the motor bearing, and it is a random gradual failure, RG. The third is the lack of or over-lubrication of the bearings of the motor. This is also a random gradual failure, RG.

The second component is the motor mounts. I have identified that the bolts could come loose. This would be an age-associated gradual failure, AG.

The third components are the sheaves. There are two failures associated with these components. First, the sheave could wear. This is an age-associated gradual failure, AG. Second, the hub for the sheave could break. This failure could be an age-associated, or a random sudden failure. (It would be a random sudden if it was not installed correctly.) However, we will assume that the hubs are installed properly; therefore, we will choose age-associated sudden failure, AS.

The fourth components are the belts. The first failure could be that the belts break due to age and wear. This is an age-associated sudden failure, AS. The second failure could be that the belts break because of improper installation, which is also an age-associated sudden failure, AS.

The fifth components are the main bearings. First, the bearings could be improperly installed, and this is random gradual failure, RG. The second and third failures are bearing failures due to high vibration and temperature. These failures are also random gradual failures, RG.

The sixth component is the shaft. The first failure could the improper material of the shaft. In the worst case, this is a random sudden failure. The second failure could be that the shaft is undersized. This could be a random sudden, or a random gradual failure. However, for this example we will choose the worst case, which is random sudden, RS.

The seventh component is the fan impeller. The first failure could be the impeller wears due to age, which is an age-associated gradual failure. The second failure could be the imbalance, which is an age-related gradual or sudden failure. In this case, we will choose the worst scenario: the age-related sudden failure, AS.

Please make sure to review this exercise again. You can also come up with more failures for each component. In cases when you are not sure whether the failure is gradual or sudden, always choose the sudden failure, which is the worst case.

Practice 3

Choose one piece of equipment in your plant and write down the components that have produced the most downtime. Categorize the type failure for each component.

1. Age-associated gradual:

2. Age-associated sudden:

3. Random gradual:

4. Random sudden:

SECTION TWO

Chapter Five

Pillars of SMR

Any solid maintenance reliability program has five fundamental pillars: management support, departmental reliability teams, training, reliability system, and success measurements.

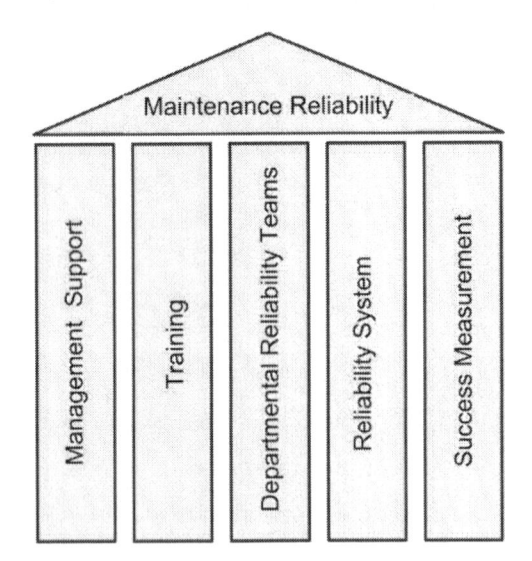

Figure 5.1. Pillars of SMR

- **Management Support:** Maintenance Reliability is a company program (and not just another maintenance plan or flavor of the month), and if implemented properly, it should become the way of life in the organization. Therefore, it must have the management support at all levels: operations, maintenance, quality, purchasing, engineering, safety, and environmental. All facets of management must come together to support this program. Most importantly, operations and maintenance must break up the supplier-customer relationship and become a team; otherwise, the journey to reliability will become frustrating and will not produce results.

- **Departmental reliability teams:** Each production department shall develop a team. The team members should include a knowledgeable production operator, production supervisor, maintenance supervisor, maintenance planner, and maintenance personnel such as mechanics and electricians.

  The team members shall choose a facilitator. Normally the facilitator is a maintenance planner or an engineer, but it could be anyone from the team. The facilitator normally organizes the meetings, keeps tabs on the activities, and follows up on the action items.

- **Training:** All management and the reliability teams must be trained on maintenance reliability. They must understand all the concepts and definitions, and how to apply them. Before undertaking any project, this training must be completed.

- **Reliability system:** The company must adopt a solid reliability system, that the team members can use and it is the same across the organization. All critical pieces of equipment shall be examined within this system and a comprehensive plan must be developed to make sure every step is taken to eliminate or prevent failures, or consequences of failures. Failures are all-inclusive, meaning equipment failures, quality issues, and performance problems.

SMR for Manufacturing Companies

In this section, you are going to learn how to make your company equipment more reliable by using the simplified maintenance reliability, also known as SMR. However, before we can define simplified maintenance reliability in detail, we must first define reliability.

In any dictionary, you would find the definition of reliability to be dependability, trustworthiness. For example, when I say my car is reliable, I mean it does not break down very often. In other words, the chances of failures are very low. Therefore, reliability is defined as chances that a component or equipment will function, as it is required without failure under specified conditions.

Now, let me define SMR. Simplified Maintenance Reliability is a simplified method to perform the steps necessary to eliminate failures or consequence of failures so the equipment could perform as required under specified conditions.

When I said my car is reliable, I did not mean that the radio worked or the seats were in perfect condition. I meant that the main functionality that was designed for is reliable. For instance, the main functionality of a foundry-molding machine is to make quality molds at a desired or designed speed.

80/20 rule

On which equipment should we use simplified maintenance reliability?

Twenty percent of the equipment cause eighty percent of the problems. This is factual, and has been proven to me many times. Let me give you an example: I started in a company as a maintenance manager. We had 150 cranes with multiple issues. It was overwhelming, and every day we had some kind of downtime that was caused by the cranes. Right away, I gave my supervisors the task of finding out which cranes produce the most downtime and were critical to the operation. After a couple of weeks, the supervisors came back with a list of critical cranes that produce the most downtime. Guess how many cranes were on that list? The number was thirty, exactly 20 percent.

What about the rest of the cranes? This is where my approach differs from the rest of the experts. Some authors do not like the 80/20 rule because they think that the rest of the equipment will go without notice. With SMR, this will not happen, as I have developed the four quadrants rule, which is also called the 4-Q rule.

4-Q Rule

Figure 5.2 represents the 4-Q rule. On the X-axis is the frequency or the occurrence of the failure. On the Y-axis is the criticality of the equipment.

This is the 4-Q rule: Twenty percent of the equipment falls within the first quadrant: highly critical and highly frequent. Thirty percent belong in the second quadrant: highly critical but low occurrence. Thirty percent fall on the third quadrant: low criticality and high frequency, and 20 percent belong to fourth quadrant: under low criticality and low occurrence.

Therefore, the SMR should first be applied to Quadrant 1, and then to the second and the third. You can also apply it to the fourth quadrant, but it needs to be justified.

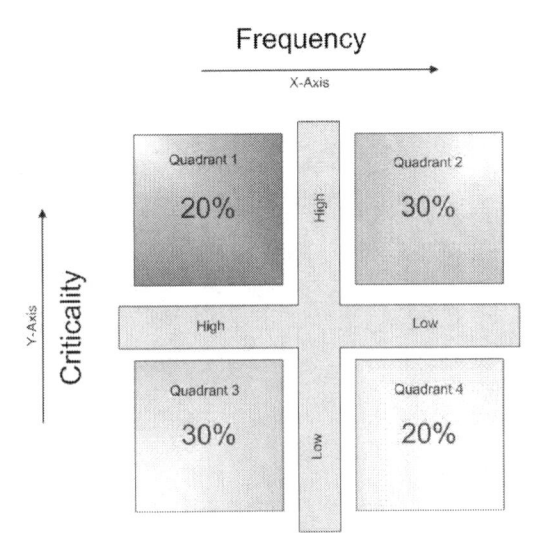

Figure 5.2. 4-Q rule

SMR Components

Figure 5.3 represents the SMR components. The first component is the type of failure. This could be one of the four types: age-associated gradual, age-associated sudden, random gradual, or random sudden.

The second component is the risk of the failure. What is the risk of this failure? The third component is the occurrence—how often the failure happens. The fourth component is the detection: How is this failure detected? The fifth component is the correct maintenance option: Based on the components 1, 2, 3, and 4, what kind of maintenance option are we going to use? This is where you will be using the maintenance option chart. The sixth component is the feasibility: Is the chosen option cost effective or implementation feasible? Finally, the seventh component is the results of the maintenance option. In other words, how would the new maintenance option eliminate or reduce the risk, frequency, and increase detection?

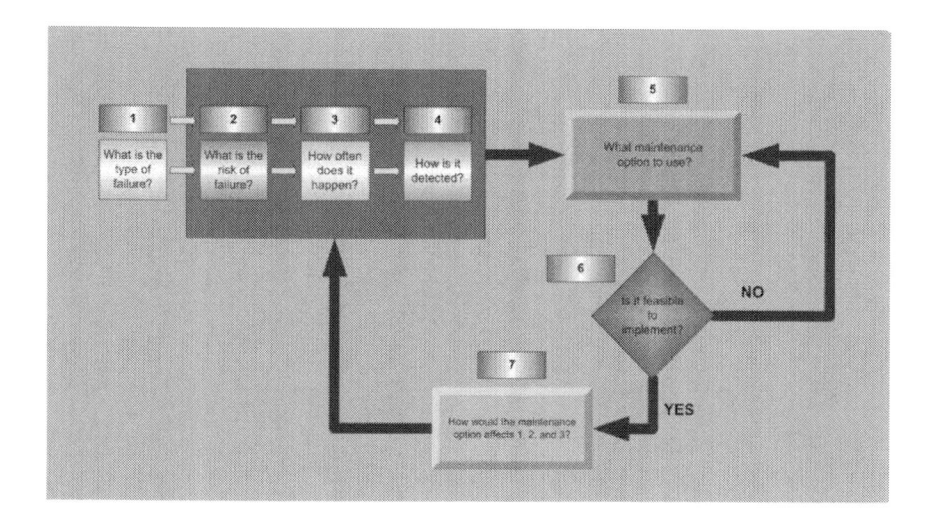

Figure 5.3. SMR components

It is important to note that normally, it is a difficult task to reduce the risk of the failure, unless there is an extensive reengineering effort. For example, if the risk is the bags breaking in a dust collector and creating an environmental issue, that risk always exists—unless a broken bag detection system is designed and installed. However, frequency can be reduced, and detection can be improved.

Later, we will be talking about SMR-FMEA, and how we can measure components 2, 3, and 4, and implement countermeasures.

Practice 4

1- Use the 80/20 rule and identify which equipment causes the most of the downtime, quality, and performance. You do not have to list the equipment in any particular order.

	Equipment
1	
2	
3	
4	
5	
6	
7	
8	
9	
10	

2- Use the four-quadrant rule and identify the equipment in Quadrants 1, 2, 3, and 4. Before doing this exercise please review the 4-Q rule in Chapter 5. You can use the chart on the next page.

Quadrant 1

	Equipment
1	
2	
3	
4	
5	
6	
7	
8	
9	
10	

Quadrant 2

	Equipment
1	
2	
3	
4	
5	
6	
7	
8	
9	
10	

Quadrant 3

	Equipment
1	
2	
3	
4	
5	
6	
7	
8	
9	
10	

Quadrant 4

	Equipment
1	
2	
3	
4	
5	
6	
7	
8	
9	
10	

Chapter 6

SMR-FMEA

Most people know what FMEA (failure mode and effect analysis) is; however, SMR-FMEA is somewhat different from the traditional failure mode and effect analysis. Therefore, I am going to explain it step by step.

First, let me define the SMR-FMEA: It is an organized technique to predict the component failures and identify actions to prevent them from occurring.

Table 6.1 shows a typical SMR-FMEA. I have divided this chart into two parts. The top of the chart contains the general information about the project, such as equipment name, team members, the date, the leader, or the facilitator. Let's assume that based on the 4-Q rule we are going to apply SMR-FMEA to the blower in the Exercise 1.

The first element is the component; for example, the motor on the blower. The second element is the potential failure mode. In other words, what could fail on this component? In the case of the motor, the first failure could be motor shorted. We also could have second or third failures: for instance, the second failure could be motor's bearing failure. Make sure you write down as many failures as possible. However, you must be logical. Make sure to include not only the failures that have occurred, but also the failures that could happen.

The third element is the type of failure. This would be one of the four types of failures: age-related gradual, age-related sudden, random gradual, or random sudden. For example, for the motor shorted, it would be age-related sudden, or AS. Here you would need the maintenance option chart discussed in Section 1.

Element number 4 is the effect of the failure. This is really the secondary failure. For example, if the blower was part of the dust collection system, the effect of the failure would be shutting down the dust collection, which would stop the operation.

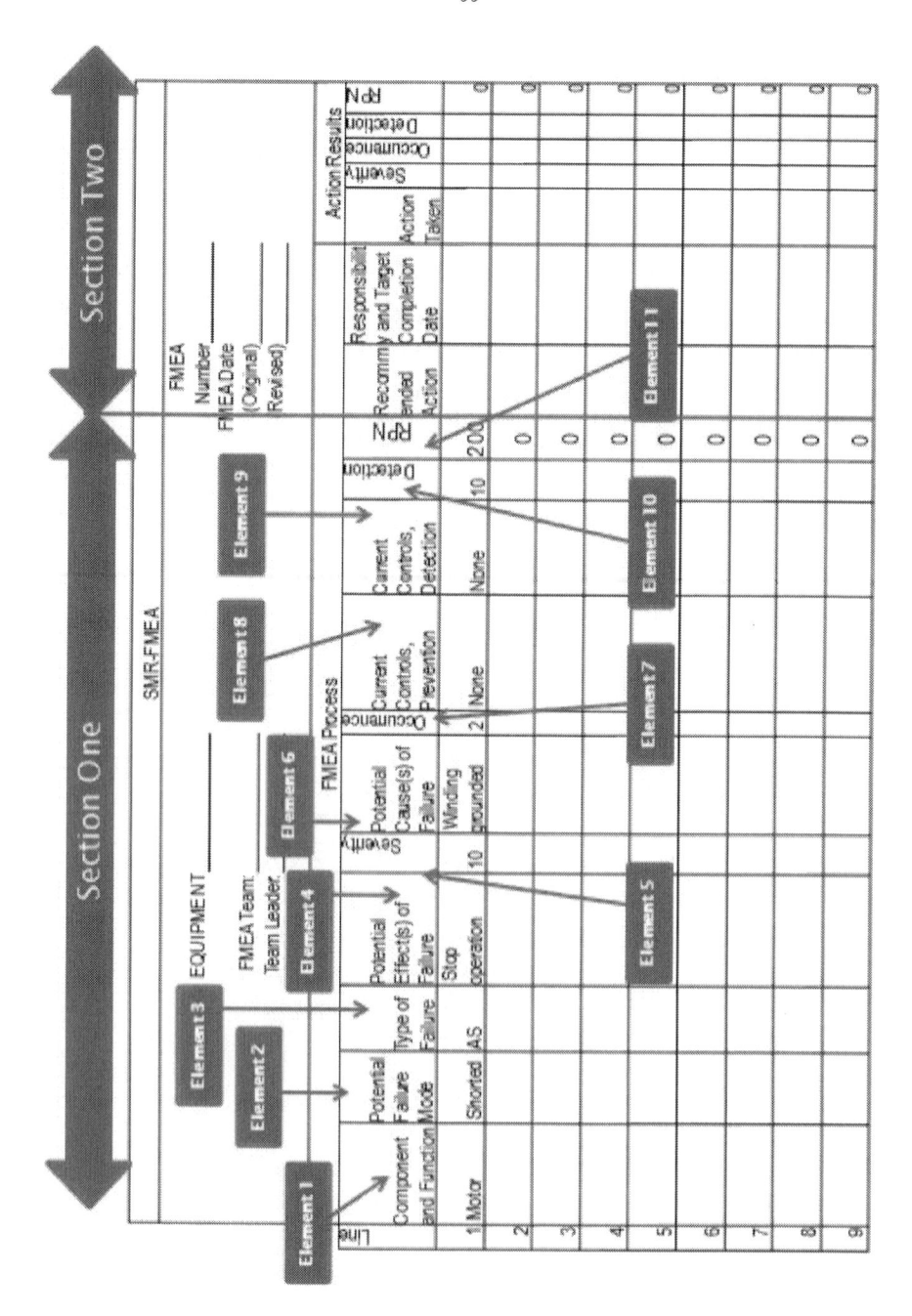

Table 6.1. SMR-FMEA elements

SMR-FMEA Analysis Worksheet

Line	Component and Function	Potential Failure Mode	Type of failure	Potential Effect(s) of Failure	Severity	Potential Cause(s) of Failure	Occurrence	Current Controls, Prevention	Current Controls, Detection	Detection	RPN	Detection/prevention option	Recommended Action	Responsibility and Target Completion Date	Action Taken	Severity	Occurrence	Detection	RPN	Comment

SMR-FMEA Team:
Team Leader:
SMR-FMEA Number:
SMR-FMEA Date:
(Revised)

SMR-FMEA Process

Action Results

The fifth element is the severity: how severe the failure is. Severity is ranked from 1 to 10: The higher the severity, the higher is the ranking. I will discuss the severity ranking later.

Element number 6 is the potential cause of the failure. For example, for the motor, it could be that the motor went to ground. Remember, this element is not really the root cause; it is about having some ideas of what went wrong.

The seventh element is the occurrence: How often does this failure happen? The ranking for occurrence is also from 1 to 10: the higher is the occurrence of the failure, the higher is the ranking number. I have developed the ranking table for the occurrence, and we will discuss it later.

Element number 8 is the current prevention methods: How do we prevent this failure right now? For example, for the motor shorted, there is no prevention method.

The ninth element is the current method of detection: How do we detect the initial failure? For example, in the case of the motor shorted, our detection could be none.

Element number 10 is the detection ranking: How do we detect the initial failure, IF? Detection is also ranked from 1 to 10. The higher is the detection ranking, the fewer detection methods. For example, if the motor shorted out, we have no detection methods. One might say the overloads would trip, and that is our detection method. However, when the overloads tripped, failure has already happened.

Element number eleven is the RPN. This is called the risk priority number, and it is the result of multiplication of the three rankings, severity, occurrence, and Detection. Therefore, the lowest number for RPN would be 1, and the highest would be 1000.

Really, the risk priority number tells us how vulnerable we are if a certain component fails. The higher the number, the more risk we are taking with a particular component.

I have specifically developed the severity, occurrence, and detection rankings for the simplified maintenance reliability.

Severity Rankings

Please look at Table 6.2, severity ranking. It is divided into five categories: very high, high, moderate, low, and very low.

Very high ranking is either 9 or 10. If the failure has an effect on safety or the environment, or involves noncompliance with the government agencies, such as EPA or OSHA, or it can endanger employees, it would have ranking of 10; however, if there is an alarm or some kind of notification present, the ranking would be reduced to a 9. For example, if the blower for the dust collector fails, this could be an environmental issue, and it should get a ranking of 10; however, if there is an alarm to notify the employees to exit the operating parameters or put on their respiratory protection equipment, the ranking would be 9.

Severity

Severity	Ranking	Criteria
Very High	9-10	Failure affects safety or involves the noncompliance to government regulations. May endanger machine assembly operator (9 with warning, 10 without warning)
High	7-8	High degree of operations dissatisfaction due to nature of the failure, such as serious disruption to process, high degree of rework and downtime
Moderate	4-5-6	Failure causes some operations dissatisfaction which may include performance deterioration, this may result in unscheduled rework/ repairs and or damage to the equipment
Low	2-3	Due to the nature of the failure operations experiences slight deterioration in performance or process.
Very Low	1	Failure would not cause any noticeable effect to operation performance, process. Operations would not be affected by this failure.

Table 6.2. Severity rankings

High severity ranking is either 7 or 8. If the failure produces a high degree of operation dissatisfaction, such as serious disruption to the process, a large amount of rework, downtime, and scrap. If the failure produces downtime or dissatisfaction, the ranking is 7; however, if it also produces rework or scrap, the ranking is 8.

Moderate ranking is 4, 5, or 6. Failure causes some degree of operations dissatisfaction that may include performance deterioration, which may result in unscheduled repairs and or damage to the equipment. The moderate ranking is more subjective, and this is why there are three numbers for this category.

Low ranking is either 3 or 2. Due to the nature of the failure, operations will likely experience a slight deterioration in performance or process. In other words, equipment still operates; however, the performance has decreased. For example, a molding machine will operate at 180 molds per hour instead of the design rate of 240.

Very low ranking is 1. Operations are not affected by the failure.

Occurrence

Occurrence ranking is an indicator of how often the failure happens, and the number is 1 through 10. Table 6.4 represents the occurrence rankings.

Ranking	Description
10	≥ 1 occurrence per shift
9	≥ 1 occurrence per day
8	≥ 1 per week
7	≥ 1 per 2 to 3 weeks
6	≥ 1 per month
5	≥ 1 per quarter
4	≥ 1 per 6 months
3	≥ 1 per year
2	≥ 1 per 2 years
1	< 1 per 3 years

Table 6.3. Occurrence ranking

The occurrence rankings are specifically designed for the simplified maintenance reliability. Since the occurrence ranking is self-explanatory, I am only going to talk about the few rankings on the chart. If the failure happens more than once per shift, the ranking is 10. For example, if we have to keep changing a component once or twice a shift, the ranking would be 10. If the failure happens less than once per month, but more than once per quarter, the ranking would be 6. If the failure were less than once per three years, the ranking would be 1. You will be using this chart extensively once you implement the simplified maintenance reliability in your plant.

Detection

Detection ranking is divided into six categories: no detection, very low, low, moderate, high, and very high.

Detection

Detection	Ranking	Detection Criteria
None	10	Controls will not or can not detect the existence of the initial failure mode. No known controls are available to detect failure mode
Very Low	9	Controls probably will not detect the existence of initial failure mode
Low	7-8	Controls have a poor chance of detecting the existence of initial failure mode.
Moderate	5-6	Controls may detect the existence of the initial failure mode
High	3-4	Controls have a good chance of detecting the initial mode. Process automatically detects failure modes.
Very High	1-2	Current controls almost certain to detect the failure mode. Reliable detection controls are known with similar processes. Process automatically detects initial failure.

Table 6.4. Detection ranking

No detection ranking is 10, and it means the current methods will not detect the initial failure, or there are no known methods available to detect it. For example, for the motor in the Exercise 1, there are no methods available to detect the motor shorting out. The only detection is the overloads or the breaker; however, the failure has already happened.

Very low detection ranking is nine, meaning current methods probably will not detect the existence of initial failure. For example, let's assume that we have a visual inspection to check for structural cracks on the molding machine. This inspection would probably not catch the initial hairline cracks.

Low detection ranking is 7 or 8. This means the current methods have a poor chance of detecting the existence of initial failure. In other words, we have some type of method in place to detect the initial failure, but most of the time the failure happens anyway. This happens mostly when the wrong maintenance option is used.

Moderate detection ranking is 5 or 6, meaning existing methods may detect the presence of the initial failure. A good example would be a motion switch on a vibratory conveyor. It may detect that conveyor overloading with materials, and send an alarm or shutdown the entire system. However, from my experience, many times the conveyers are overloaded with materials already, before the switch can detect the initial failure.

High detection ranking is 3 or 4. This means existing methods have a good chance of detecting the initial failure. For example, in Exercise 1, if we install a proper vibration switch on the bearings, we would have a good chance of detecting when the vibration reaches the set point. Obviously, the vibration switch should be set accordingly to detect the initial failure.

Very high detection ranking is 1 or 2. This means that the current method almost certain to detect the initial failure or detection is automatically built into the process. For example, in Exercise 1, if we install an automatic vibration sensor instead of a vibration switch that can sense the vibration of the bearings continuously, we would be almost certain that we could detect the initial failure of the bearings due to vibration as long as the sensor works properly.

You do not have to memorize these materials. However, you must be able to use them once you implement simplified maintenance reliability in your plant.

RPN

As I mentioned before, RPN is the result of multiplication of severity, occurrence, and detection. The maximum RPN value is 1000, and the minimum is 1. Any component with a RPN of more than 48 needs special attention.

Many people ask me why I have chosen the RPN of 48 as the threshold number. The answer is, if you refer back to the severity, occurrence, and detection charts, this would give you a severity of 4, occurrence of 4, and detection of 3. You can change this RPN limit to a lower or a higher number. However, 48 (or rounding it to 50) has worked properly in identifying the risk of failures that need to be addressed.

Regardless of the RPN, special attention should be given to components with severity of 9 and 10. Remember, these are components that can cause injuries, death, safety, or environmental issues. If the failure has not occurred yet, assume a 1 for the occurrence.

Regardless of the detection, if the severity and occurrence are both greater than 8, this means there are design issues with the component or the process. For example, if the bags are breaking in a bag-house every day and produce an environmental issue, this is no more a maintenance problem—it is a design issue. It could be the velocity of the dust entering the bag-house, bags are too close to the inlet of the collector, or parameters such as air to cloth ratio, can velocity, or the material of the bags.

I'm not talking about the components that must be maintained daily. For example, the nitrogen filter in the pressurized holding furnace might have to be replaced once a shift by the operator or the maintenance personnel. That is understandable and might have been part of the design. However, if the same filter had to be changed every half hour during the production, and created unnecessary downtime, this is a design issue, and it could be caused by many design parameters.

SMR-FMEA, Section 2

Now let us discuss Section 2 of the SMRFMEA. Table 6.5 represents Section 2 of the SMR-FMEA.

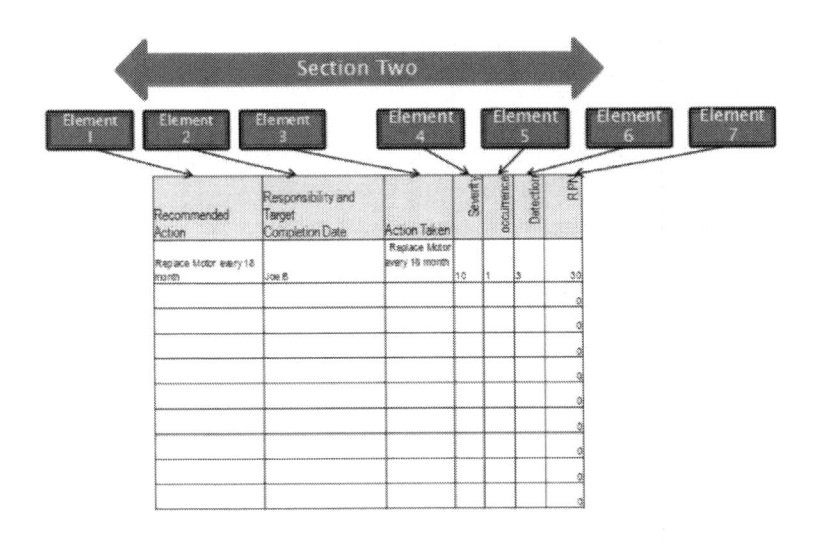

Table 6.5. Section 2 of SMR-FMEA

Element 1 is the recommended action. This is really the maintenance option we would choose based on the type of failure. For this element, you must use the maintenance option in Chapter 4 (Table 4.1). For example, if the failure is age-related gradual, AG, you should use one of the five options that are available and appropriate for this type of failure. Any other recommendation is not acceptable.

Let's look at the motor in the Exercise 1. We know one of the failures was the motor shorted, and we determined this was an age-related sudden failure. Please look at the maintenance option chart in Chapter 4. There are four options available; however, only two are viable. One is the time-based replacement; the other is the redundant system. As you well know, we cannot have a redundant motor on one blower. Therefore, the only redundancy would be a second new blower system with fan and the motor. We might not be able to justify this option financially, however. The only option would be the timed-based replacement of the motor. Let's say this motor only lasted two years. With the timed-based replacement, we will replace this motor every eighteen to twenty months, and we would refurbish the old motor or purchase a new one.

Element 2 is the responsibility and target completion date. This is self-explanatory. In other words, who is going to perform this action and what is the estimated completion date?

Element 3 is what exact action we are taking. For instance, this could be changing the motor every eighteen months.

Element 4, 5, 6, and 7 are the severity, occurrence, detection, and the RPN numbers for the new maintenance option that is taken. We would still use the same charts that we used before.

Here is where SMR-FMEA differs from the traditional failure mode and effect analysis. In traditional FMEA, the new severity, occurrence, and detection are not completed until we have experienced some validation data from our action. For example, in case of the motor, we should wait three or more years to validate weather our action of replacing the motor every eighteen months has worked. Then we can calculate the new RPN number. This is not the case for the SMR-FMEA. In most cases, we can complete this section immediately. There are two reasons for this.

First, we are simply making predictions and not validations of the results. Since the SMR-FMEA is a working document, and we keep going back to fine-tune it, if our countermeasure does not meet our expectation, we would review it again and find out why. Most likely, we chose an incorrect maintenance option or the type of failure.

Second, in many cases it is difficult to reduce the severity because it will most likely require a redesign and cannot be financially justified. In the motor example, this motor could be part of a blower to a bag-house for the company's sand system, and when the motor fails, the dust pollution in the company could create a safety concern. This could be in form of respiratory or visibility issues, and the company operation could stop. Therefore, to reduce the severity, we must design and install a redundant fan system. However, the redundant system might not be easily justified. As a result, replacing the motor every eighteen months would be the best economical option; nevertheless, this will not reduce the severity for the reason that if the motor fails, we still would have the same safety issues. Thus, only the occurrence and detection numbers can be reduced. In this case, occurrence would change to 1 because we are predicting that the motor will not fail during the operation since it is replaced every eighteen months, and detection would become 3, because we are predicting that the failure would not happen during the eighteen-month period.

Now if we plug in these numbers as I discussed, we would get a RPN of 30, which is less than 48.

Table 6.6 shows Section 1 of the SMR-FMEA of the blower example.

Line	Component and Function	Potential Failure Mode	TYPE OF FAILURE	Potential Effect(s) of Failure	Severity	Potential Cause(s) of Failure	Occurrence	Current Controls, Prevention	Current Controls, Detection	Detection	RPN
1	Motor	Motor grounded/shorted	AS	Safety, stops operation	10	Motor shorted	2	None	None	10	200
2		Bearing failure	RG	Safety, stops operations	10	Bearing vibration	3	None	None	10	300
3		Lack or over Lube of bearing	RG	Safety, stops operation	10	Over lube/under Lube (training)	1	Check once/shift	Check once/shift	1	10
4	Motor mounts	One come loose	AG	Could cause other break	7	Low vibration/worn threads	1	Check once/shift	Check once/shift	1	10
5	Sheaves	Worn	AG	Improper speed/belt loose	5	Age, improper PM	3	None	None	10	150
6		Hub breaking	AS	Safety, Stop operation	7	Improper installation	1	None	None	10	70
7	Belt	Belt break	AG	Safety, stop operation	10	Age,	3	None	None	10	300
8		Belt break	AS	Safety, stop operation	8	Improper install (loose belts)	3	None	None	10	240
9	Main bearings	Bearings failing	RG	Safety, stop operation	10	Improper install	1	None	Laser alignment and final inspection	3	30
10		Bearings Failure	RG	Safety, stop operation	10	High vibration	2	None	Monthly check	5	100
11		Bearings Failure	RG	Safety, stop operation	10	High Temperature	2		Monthly check	3	60
12	Shaft	Shaft failing	RS	Safety, stop operation	10	Shaft materials	1	Check material before installation	Check material prior to installation	1	10
13		Shaft failing	RG/RS	Safety, stop operation	10	Shaft undersized	1	Shaft size check prior to install	Check shaft size prior to install	1	10
14	Fan impeller	Impeller worn	AG	Performance decrease	5	Age, improper PM	1	Yearly :check impeller dim	Yearly: check impeller dim	1	5
15		Imbalance	AS	Safety, stop operation	10	Age, improper PM	2	Monthly balance check	Monthly balance check	7	140

Table 6.6. Section 1 of the blower example

Let's also assume that this equipment is the blower for the company's dust collector. In addition, we have some downtime history.

The history does not need to be very accurate as long as we can assign some reasonable occurrence numbers.

The motor is the first component. The first failure could be the motor grounded or shorted out. I assigned AS as the type of failure, meaning this is an age-related sudden. I also assigned the severity of 10, because the collector would not run, and the operation would stop. Based on the history, the occurrence is 2, meaning the failure happens every two years. Since we cannot detect the initial failure, the detection is 10, and as the result, the RPN is 200.

The second motor failure is the random gradual RG and was due to high vibration. Again, the severity is 10; however, this failure has happened more than once in two years, therefore the occurrence is 3, and since we currently have no detection methods, the detection would be 10, and as the result, the RPN for this failure is 300.

The third motor failure could be the lack or over lube of the motor bearings, and normally a training issue. The severity for this failure is still 10, because bearings could heat up, and cause the motor to trip the overloads, which would stop the operation. However, the occurrence is 1, meaning we have no history, or it only has occurred once in more than three years. Since we inspect the bearing lubrication every shift, the detection is 1, and as the result, the RPN is 10.

Let's examine another failure. Please look at line number 7. This is the belt failure. I have chosen an age-related sudden for this failure. The severity is still 10, because the operation stops and it is time consuming to replace them. Since this failure happens more than once per year, the occurrence is 3. Our current method of detection does not catch the initial failure; therefore, the detection is 10 and as the result, the RPN is 300.

Please make sure that you review the entire SMR-FMEA for the previous example, along with the maintenance options, severity, occurrence and detection charts.

SMR-FMEA, Section Two, Blower Example

Table 6.7 shows the completed Section 2 of the SMR-FMEA for the blower example. Please make sure to refer back to the severity, ranking, and detection charts.

The motor had three failures. The first failure was the motor grounded or shorted, and we decided this was an age-associated sudden failure AS. For this, I have chosen the option of timed-based replacement. We would change the motor with new or a rebuild unit every eighteen months. Remember, when we completed the first section of SMR-FMEA for this motor, we had chosen an occurrence of 2, meaning it fails every couple of years. Therefore, by replacing it every eighteen months, the failure should not happen. Thus, the severity stays the same, occurrence will be 1, detection becomes 3, and as the result, the new RPN becomes 30.

Line	Component and Function	Potential Failure Mode	Type of Failure	Recommended Action	Responsibility and Target Completion Date	Action Taken	Severity	Occurrence	Detection	RPN
1	Motor	Motor grounded/ shorted	AS	Replace motor every 18 months	Joe M.	Replace motor every 18 month, and modify PM	10	1	1	10
2		Bearing failure	RG	Install vibration monitor and	Dale C.	Install vibration monitor and	10	1	1	10
3		Lack or over Lube of bearing	RG	Existing action		Existing action	10	1	1	10
4	Motor mounts	One come loose	AG	Existing action		Existing action	10	1	1	10
5	Sheaves	Worn out	AG	Replace sheaves every 18 months, when motor replaced	Joe M.	Replace motor every 18 months	10	1	1	10
6		Hub breaking	AS	Training	Fred B.	Training on proper install, final	10	1	1	10
7	Belts	Belt break	AG	Replace belts every 4 months	Joe M	replace belts every 4 months	10	1	1	10
8		Belt break/ installation	RS	Training	Fred B.	Training on proper installation of belts/ final inspection for loose belts	10	1	1	10
9	Main bearings	Bearings failing	RG	Existing action		Existing action	10	1	3	30
10		Bearings Failure	RG	Vibration monitor / trend	Dale C	Vibration monitor / trend	10	1	1	10
11		Bearings Failure	RG	Install temperature monitoring/	Dale C	Install temperature monitoring	10	1	1	10
12	Shaft	Shaft failing	RS	Existing action		Existing Action	10	1	1	10
13		Shaft failing	RG/RS	Existing Action		Existing Action	10	1	1	10
14	Fan impeller	Impeller worn	AG	Existing action		Existing action	5	1	1	5
15		Imbalance	AS	Install Vibration monitoring		Install vibration monitoring / re-	10	1	1	10

Table 6.7. Section 2 of the SMR-FMEA for the blower

Next would be the bearing failure of the motor, a random gradual failure. For this option, I selected the event-based maintenance. We would install a vibration-monitoring device to detect the initial vibration of the bearings. Again, the severity stays the same; however, the occurrence and detection become one, because we can detect the initial failure due to vibration with the new vibration monitoring system. As the result, the new RPN becomes 10.

For the lack of lube or over lube, we are keeping our existing maintenance program, as it is working, and the original RPN was 10, which is a very low number.

Let us look at another example, the V-belts. Belts could break due to improper installation, and this is an age-associated sudden failure. The original RPN for this failure was 300. For this failure, I selected proper V-belt installation training. Again, severity stays the same; however, the occurrence and the detection become 1. Because we have trained our personnel during the installation, we will inspect to ensure the belts are installed properly and the tension is correct. Thus, the new RPN becomes 10.

Please review Table 6.7 again. Make sure to follow the same logic as I have explained here and familiarize yourself with the options that I have chosen, and how I calculated the new RPNs. You can visit www.simplified-maintenance-reliability.com and download SMR-FMEA templates and print out severity, detection, occurrence, and option charts.

Practice 5

1- What was the first equipment?

2- Start a SMR-FMEA for the above equipment. Identify the components, determine the type of failures, severity, occurrence, and detection, and then calculate the RPNs.

Line	Component and Function	Potential Failure Mode	Type of Failure	Potential Effect(s) of Failure	Severity	Potential Cause(s) of Failure	Occurrence	Current Controls, Prevention	Current Controls, Detection	Detection	RPN
1											
2											
3											
4											
5											
6											
7											
8											
9											
10											
11											
12											
13											
14											
15											
16											
17											

3- Note the RPNs that are over 50. Use Section 2 of the SMR-FMEA; create a recommended action for each component that has a RPN greater than 50. Make sure you calculate the new RPNs, and the recommended action that would produce a RPN 50 or less. Use the chart on the next page.

Recommended Action	Responsibility / Target Completion Date	Action Taken	Severity	Occurrence	Detection	RPN	Coments

Chapter Seven

Implementing SMR

One thing that everyone should understand is that SMR is a team approach and cannot be completed by one individual in the organization.

The first team member should be a facilitator; this individual is normally a maintenance engineer, planner, or a supervisor. The second member should be a qualified production operator, meaning an operator who knows the process, and can fully explain the operation of the system. Other members should be maintenance and operation supervisors, maintenance superintendents, and one or two repairpersons, such as electricians and mechanics. Prior to start of the project, all team members should have gone through this training. If other experts are needed such as mechanical, electrical, or process engineers, you can include them as part of the team or request their help as needed.

Facilitator's Role

1. Coordinate the meetings.

2. Work with the team to prioritize the projects.

3. Make sure the SMR process is being followed.

4. Set up tours of the equipment.

5. Complete the SMR-FMEA using the team members' input.

6. Make sure the actions on the SMRFMEA are being implemented.

7. Make sure everyone's roles and project responsibilities are defined.

8. Get other experts to help with the projects when needed.

9. Set up review meetings.

Ten Safety Checks That Must Be Completed before Moving to the SMR-FMEA

1. Knowing the source of energy.

2. Knowing where we lock out the source directly.

3. Knowing what the other sources of energies are.

4. Knowing where the other sources of energies are.

5. Validating that the system is at zero state of energy.

6. Having a comprehensive lock-out tag-out procedure.

7. Making sure that everyone is trained on this procedure.

8. Evidence of training.

9. Evidence that arc flash study has been completed.

10. Checking with your safety and environmental for other procedures related to safety and environmental policies.

Typical SMR Project

A typical SMR project takes about three to four weeks; however, not all the action items are completed during this period. As you well know, some projects require ordering parts or capital budget approvals, which could take many weeks or months. By completing the project, I mean that the SMR-FMEA is completed, and everyone's responsibility is defined.

The first meeting should last about one hour. Teams should use the 4-Q rule and make a comprehensive list of equipment in Quadrants 1 and 2. Then the team should prioritize the equipment in each quadrant, and choose the first project in the first quadrant.

The second meeting is about two hours. Prior to the meeting, the facilitator should develop a component list. For this list, he or she can use the SMR-FMEA, or a different list that can later be imported. In addition, the team shall take a tour of the equipment and fully understand the process and the problems. Normally, a knowledgeable production operator or a supervisor who is part of the team is the tour guide. This is the best opportunity for team members to familiarize themselves with equipment and the components. If other experts are needed such as mechanical, electrical, or process engineers, you can include them as part of the team or request their help as needed. The team should gather in a meeting room, and complete the ten safety checks. If the checklist is not satisfactory, the facilitator should assign an action on the action items list, and assign it to the correct individual. Next, the team should start the SMR-FMEA, complete Section 1, and calculate the existing RPNs.

The third meeting is about two hours. Team should use the maintenance option chart and choose the right action for each component that has a RPN greater than 50, and assign individuals to each project. Next, the team should recalculate the RPNs and make sure that all the new results are less than 50. Subsequently, the team should evaluate the PMs that need to be revised. All efforts should be made to put into practice 40 to 50 percent conditional maintenance. If there are trainings that are identified in the SMR-FMEA, the team should make sure they are scheduled.

Action Items List

Once you implement simplified maintenance reliability in your plant, you could be working on several SMR-FMEAs at the same time. Even though it is not mandatory, I suggest having a separate action items list on all the projects. This way, you have a current list of all the actions that can easily be reviewed occasionally. Every time I complete an SMR-FMEA, I make sure to add the recommended actions to the action items list. Table 7.1 represents a typical action item list.

Item #	Action	Responsible	Start date	Complete Date	Comments

Table 7.1. Action items list

Hidden Failures

Hidden failure is defined as a failure that goes undetected until it is uncovered by another event or failure. Let me explain this with an example.

Please look at Figure 7.1. Suppose from the SMR-FMEA, we have determined that we need to install a redundant proximity switch for the carriage return travel.

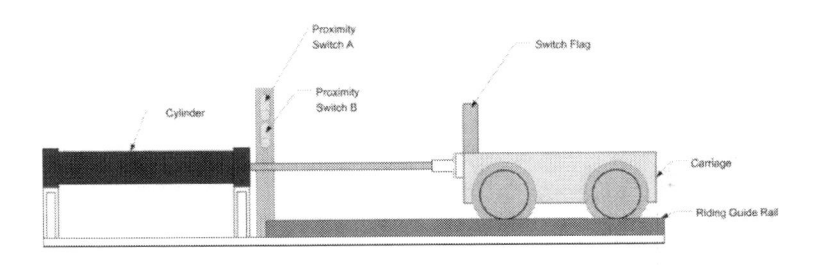

Figure 7.1. Redundancy and hidden failures

When the carriage retracts both proximity switches are energized, indicating the carriage is returned; however, if one of the switches fails, for instance proximity switch A, the system would still function properly, and the switch failure would go unnoticed. This is a hidden failure.

It is important to make sure that we can detect hidden failures. For the example above, since both switches have to be energized at the same time, we can include a notification in our controls that when one switch is energized and the other is not, an error message is displayed. Not every hidden failure can be detected in this manner;, some of them must be detected by regular inspections. Figure 7.2a represents a simple electrical circuit. Once the contact is made, the buzzer would sound. Let us assume this was a circuit for a fire alarm, and we have had issues with the contact corrosion: the buzzer did not sound when we had a small fire. Therefore, we decide to install a redundant parallel contact to ensure that we have two contacts in case of corrosion.

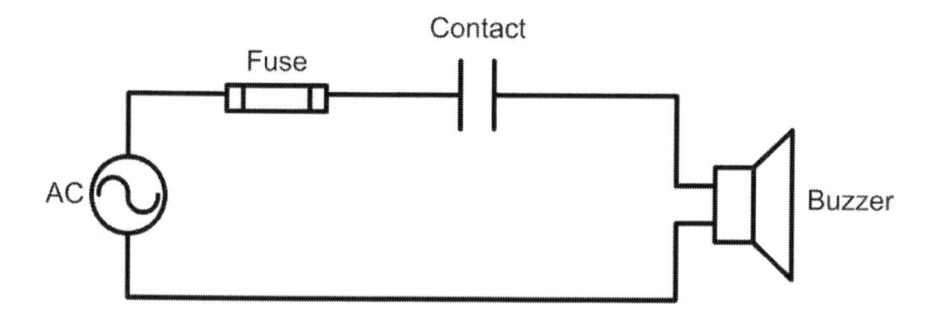

Figure 7.2a. Fire alarm circuit

    Figure 7.2b shows the alarm circuit with a secondary contact, B. Now if contact A fails, contact B can still carry the current and energize the buzzer. In fact, the only way that the buzzer would not sound would be if both contacts were corroded; however, if one of the contacts fails, we have no way of detecting it. For this example, regular inspection of the contacts would ensure that failure is detected.

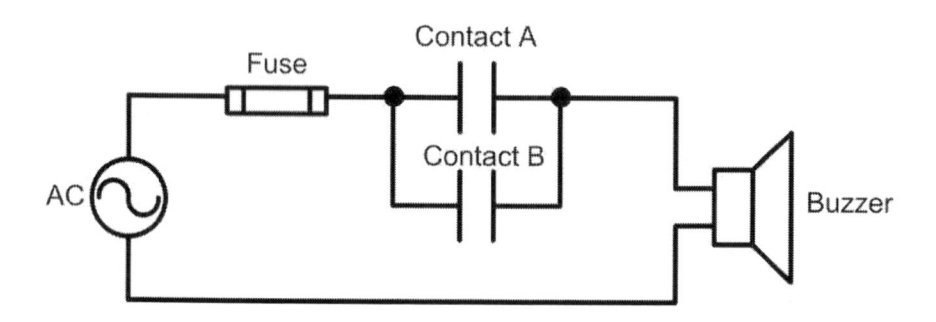

Figure 7.2b. Alarm circuit with redundant contacts

Nine Important Details to Remember

1. Make sure the correct maintenance option is chosen.

2. Make sure the correct type of failure is selected.

3. Make sure any component with a RPN of over 50 has a correct countermeasure.

4. If the failure is random sudden, regular time-based inspection, or overhauling the equipment will not produce results.

5. Always make sure you have a maintenance program associated with the hidden failures.

6. The goal should be to drive the maintenance program to 40 percent conditional maintenance.

7. If the RPN is over 50, and the action is to keep the existing PM program, this is not acceptable. A few years ago, I was reviewing a SMR-FMEA, one of the components had a RPN of 400, and the action was to keep the existing PM. Therefore, I told the team if the existing PM program were working, the RPN would not be 400. This is like saying, "I know I'm having a heart attack, but I'm not going to do anything about it." Remember this: If your existing program is working, the RPN would not be high, and you would not need to use these methods.

8. If the failure is still occurring, make sure to refer back to the SMR-FMEA. Most likely, the type of the failure or the maintenance option you have chosen is incorrect.

9. As I have said before, it is a difficult task to reduce the severity. Sometimes it cannot be justified, or it would require a major reengineering. However, our first and most important goal should be to reduce the severity. If the method to reduce the severity is proved not to be feasible by management, then we should concentrate on drastically reducing occurrence and detection numbers.

Chapter Eight

Measuring Results

People are the greatest assets in any company, and their time is valuable. Therefore, any program that is implemented in any organization must show positive and measurable results. Otherwise, these programs are useless, and all they become fluff and bluff, or dog and pony shows that do not amount to anything. In addition, the correct way of measuring results will point to the right direction, whether you need to modify the program, retain it, or eliminate it. I have chosen a few metrics that allows you to measure the success of the SMR program.

Overall Equipment Effectiveness (OEE)

Any equipment or system is required to perform to desired or specified results. For example, a purchased press is required to produce three hundred pressed products per hour with maximum of 1 percent scrap. Three major factors affect the overall effectiveness of the press. The first one is known as availability. Availability means how often machine is ready to run or available. Therefore, availability is the total machine time minus the downtime, including planned and unplanned, divided by total machine time.

$$\text{Availability} = \frac{\text{Total Time Available - Total Downtime}}{\text{Total Time Available}} \times 100$$

Example: A 200-ton press is required to run twenty-four hours per day, seven days per week. The equipment requires eighteen hours of planned maintenance and eight hours of unplanned downtime. Therefore, the availability is calculated as:

$$\{[(24 \times 7)-(18+8)] / (24 \times 7)\} \times 100 = 84.5 \text{ percent}$$

In the above example, the machine is available to run 84.5 percent of the time, or 15.5 percent of the time the machine is not available because of downtime.

The second factor is the performance. When the equipment is available, does it perform to the desired cycle time? For example, the press is designed to produce 300 pieces per hour, and the availability is 85.5 percent. Therefore, the total possible pieces that can be produced in twenty-four hours would be 6156 pieces. However, the machine produces 5700 pieces. Therefore, press produced 238 pieces per hour, which is 5700 divided by 24. This is also known as effective cycle. The mathematical equation for performance is:

$$\text{Performance} = \frac{\text{Total units Produced}}{\text{Total possible units when machine is available}} \times 100$$

Based on the above equation, the performance for the press example calculated:

$$(5700/6156) \times 100 = 92.6 \text{ percent}$$

Some of the reasons for performance losses are machine setups, frequent start stops, machine slowdowns because of quality problems, and waiting for samples or test results such as hardness or chemistry.

The third factor is quality, which is measured as number of good units divided by the total number of units produced.

$$Quality = \frac{\text{Number of Pieces Produced} - \text{Number of Defective Pieces}}{\text{Total Number of Pieces Produced}} \times 100$$

In the press example, let us assume that the press produced three hundred defective parts. Therefore, the quality is calculated as:

$$[(5700-300) / 5700] \times 100 = 94.7 \text{ percent}$$

Now that we know availability, performance, and quality, we can define the Overall Equipment Effectiveness (OEE). OEE is the multiplication of availability performance and quality.

OEE = Availability x Performance x Quality

For the press example, the OEE would be:

Press OEE= 84.5 percent x 92.6 percent x 94.7 percent= 74.1 percent

As is obvious, OEE measurement identifies how effective your equipment is operating. The whole focus of SMR is to improve OEE. Identifying potential failures, occurrence, detection, and developing solutions to eliminate failures and equipment slowdowns are the keys to improving OEE. Remember, as I have mentioned before, bad quality is also considered as a failure.

Another great benefit of OEE is benchmarking against the world-class companies. The OEE for a world-class company is 85 percent. It is the result of availability at 90 percent, performance at 95 percent, and quality at 99 percent.

OEE of World-Class Company= 90% (Availability) x 95% (Performance) x 99% (Quality)

Each company shall develop methods to calculate the OEE for all equipment or systems. This measurement should be recorded daily, weekly, monthly, and quarterly. The goal should be to improve the OEE to reach 85 percent. Figure 8.1a shows the OEE for seven days of press performance. You can develop your own charts that make more sense for the company's particular operation. In addition to the chart, the sources of downtime, planned and unplanned, as well as performance and quality issues shall be identified and corrected using SMR methods.

PRESS OEE

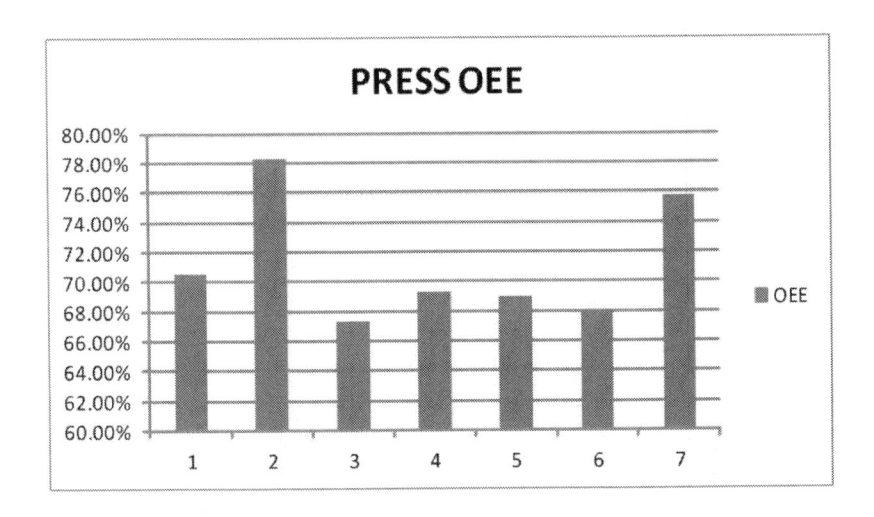

Figure 8.1a. Press OEE for seven days

Now that we have developed the OEE for the press, we must make sure we are capturing and documenting the reasons for all the downtimes for availability, performance, and quality issues. Using these documents, we shall develop Pareto charts for elements that make up the OEE, meaning availability, performance, and quality. Figure 8.1b shows an example of the Pareto for the availability of the press as a percentage of the total downtime.

Press Availability Pareto

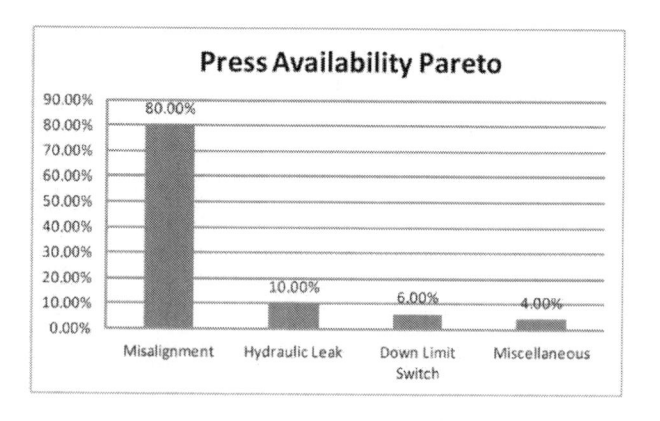

Misalignment	80.00%
Hydraulic Leak	10.00%
Down Limit Switch	6.00%
Miscellaneous	4.00%

Figure 8.1b. Press availability Pareto

Based on Figure 8.1b, we have determined that 80 percent of the total downtime is caused by the misalignment. Let us assume that we had completed a SMR project on this press six months ago, and all the action items are completed. Either the press misalignment is a new problem that we did not include in our SMR-FMEA, or it is an old problem with a wrong maintenance option. In any case, we should go back, review the SMR-FMEA, and make sure we are addressing the misalignment issue correctly. We should make sure that the RPN is correct; if not, we should check the severity, occurrence, and detection numbers and recalculate the RPN. Next, we have to make sure that we use the option chart in Chapter 4 and choose the right option. By continuously checking the OEE and referring back to the SMR-FMEA, we are always in a continuous improvement mode.

Remember the seventh component of the SMR. Does the countermeasure affect the RPN? If it does not improve the RPN to less than 50, we must come up with a new maintenance option.

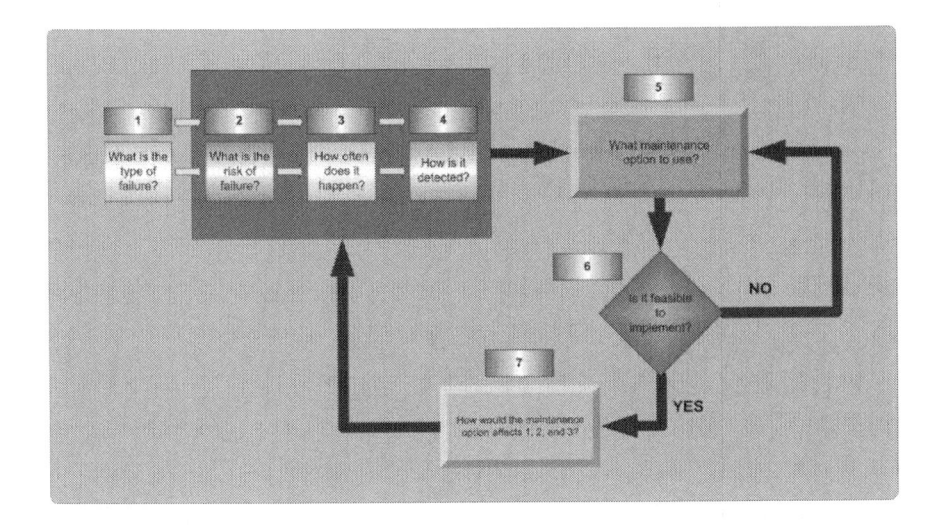

Figure 8.2. SMR components

Remember, the only options that are available to maintenance are the ones that I have explained in Chapter 4; therefore, there is no need for extensive studies and six-sigma projects. Even if you start a six-sigma project on a maintenance issue at the end of the project, you would end up using one of the options in the option chart. Therefore, it is much easier to complete the SMR-FMEA and use methods that I have explained so far.

Estimated Replacement Value (ERV)

I am sure someone in your organization is telling you that you are spending too much, and need to cut down on your maintenance spending. I am also sure you have a spending budget in your organization. However, do you really know what is the correct maintenance spending for a company of your size?

ERV is the percentage of the total maintenance cost including labor and materials, divided by the estimated replacement value of the company. Figure 8.3 represents this calculation. The key is to know the value of the company each year. In other words, we should know how much capital it takes to build the company from ground up. For example, if the ERV of your company was 50 million dollars last year and you spent 2.5 million in total labor and materials, the ERV for last year would be 5 percent.

$$ERV\% = \frac{\text{Total Maintenance Cost}}{\text{Estimated Replacement Value}} \times 100$$

Figure 8.3. ERV percent calculation

Example 9.1:

$$ERV\% = \frac{2.5 \text{ Million}}{50 \text{ Million}} \times 100 = 5\%$$

In most companies, the accounting department would have the estimated value of the company, or you can sit down and calculate the value based on the assets including the buildings, foundations, and the equipment. You can also hire an industrial appraisal company to calculate the estimated value of the company. They can also recalculate the value, based on improvements, new capital projects, and inflation. ERV for a typical company is 3.5 to 5 percent; however, a correctly managed maintenance department runs about 3 to 3.5 percent. On the other hand, a world-class company has an ERV value of 2.5 to 3 percent. This number will inform you whether you are over or under spending. If the ERV is less than 2.5 percent, you are most likely under spending, and result would be higher downtime and emergency work-orders. What ERV number does not tell you is where the problem is—is it in the labor or material cost? Therefore, you must have other sets of measurements to identify the problem. I will discuss these measurements later in this chapter. Figure 8.4 represents the ERV chart for a typical manufacturing company.

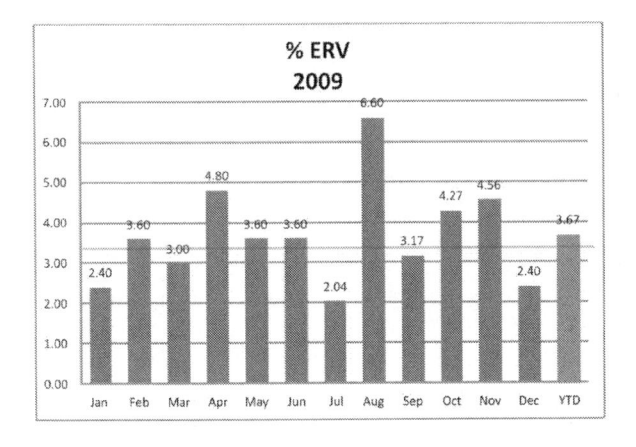

Figure 8.4. ERV chart for a typical company

You should review the ERV on monthly basis. Make sure you always set a goal for the ERV; a typical goal should be about 3.5 percent. If your maintenance ERV is 5 percent or higher, your maintenance department is out of control; either you have too many people, or no one is controlling the material cost. Make sure you set an achievable goal. If your ERV percent is 5 percent, you should set a goal of 4.25 percent. Once the SMR is properly implemented in your company, you will start noticing a decrease in ERV percentage. This could take up to two years. If you decrease the ERV immediately by not purchasing materials and reducing headcount, you could end up having more failures—that could be catastrophic. Remember, by implementing SMR, the ERV will decrease automatically, because you are making the equipment more reliable. Make sure you discuss the gradual decrease of the ERV percent with your management, so expectations are not set so high that they would be impossible to achieve.

Types of Work-Orders

There are four types of work-orders: planned, corrective, unplanned, and emergency. As the name implies, planned work-orders are PMs, or planned shutdown work that is scheduled by the maintenance department. A corrective work-order is a job that needs some kind of repair or replacement, but the problem has not caused a major issue. The example could be a low-level vibration indication on a bearing. An unplanned work-order is normally written for a problem that has caused some degree of dissatisfaction for operation; however, operation has tolerated the issue but the problem needs to be corrected within the next forty-eight hours. An emergency work-order is written for a job that has caused a high degree of dissatisfaction inform of downtime, rework, an environmental, or a safety issue and must be addressed immediately. Figure 8.5 represents an example of the work-order category chart.

Type	Jan	Feb	Mar	Apr	May	Jun	July	Aug	Sep	Oct	Nov	Dec
Planned	30.00%	50.00%	52.00%	48.00%	38.00%	50.00%	50.00%	60.00%	60.00%	60.00%	65.00%	70.00%
Corrective	50.00%	30.00%	32.00%	32.00%	42.00%	40.00%	38.00%	30.00%	30.00%	31.00%	26.00%	25.00%
Unplanned	10.00%	10.00%	9.00%	8.00%	12.00%	3.00%	6.00%	4.00%	6.00%	5.50%	6.50%	3.00%
Emergency	10.00%	10.00%	7.00%	12.00%	8.00%	7.00%	6.00%	6.00%	4.00%	3.50%	2.50%	2.00%
	100.00%	100.00%	100.00%	100.00%	100.00%	100.00%	100.00%	100.00%	100.00%	100.00%	100.00%	100.00%

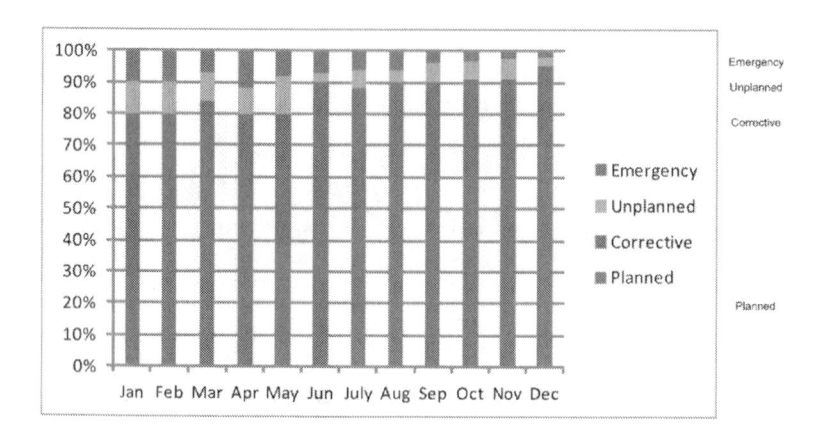

Figure 8.5. Types of work-orders

Notice that in the above example, the work-orders are shown in percentages as a total number of work-orders. The goal should be to drive the unplanned and emergencies to zero percent. Obviously, zero percent is idealistic. A reasonable goal should be less than 5 percent.

The work-order type chart is a very good indicator of how the simplified maintenance reliability is performing. As you complete SMR in different parts of the plant, the percentage of emergency and unplanned work-orders shall decrease.

Work-Order Backlog

Work-order backlog is another measurement that must be closely examined. A typical company carries four weeks of work-order backlog. This is measured is by dividing the number of work-orders in the backlog by the average number of work-orders completed in one week. Figure 8.6 represents the calculation for the average number of work-orders per week (ANW).

$$\text{AVE. \# of work-orders per week (ANW)} = \frac{\text{Number of work-orders completed in (N) weeks}}{N}$$

Figure 8.6. Average number of work-orders per week

Example: The maintenance department has completed six hundred work-orders in ten weeks. Therefore, the average number of completed work-orders per week are calculated as:

$$\text{ANW} = 600/10 = 60$$

Once we know the average number of completed work-orders per week, we can calculate the number of weeks of work-order backlog. Work-order backlog in weeks is calculated by dividing the total number of work-orders in backlog divided by the average number of work-orders completed per week.

$$\text{Weeks of Backlog} = \frac{\text{Total Number of Work-orders in the Backlog}}{\text{ANW}}$$

	Jan	Feb	Mar	Apr	May	Jun	Jul	Aug	Sep	Oct	Nov	Dec
Number of Workorders	400	300	300	400	600	300	260	240	210	200	240	210
ANW	60	60	60	60	60	60	60	60	60	60	60	60
Weeks of Backlog	6.7	5.0	5.0	6.7	10.0	5.0	4.3	4.0	3.5	3.3	4.0	3.5

Figure 8.7. Backlog in weeks

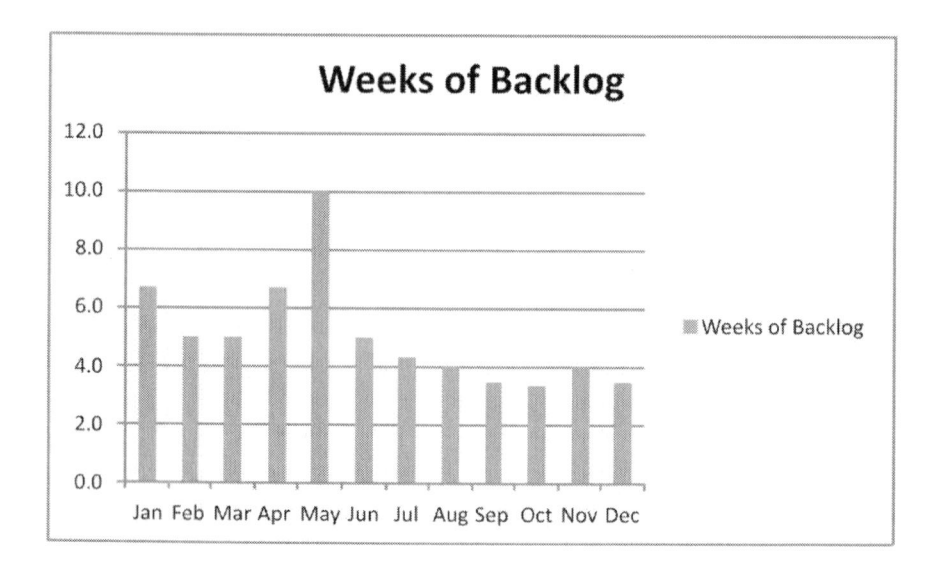

Figure 8.8. Weeks of backlog

Figure 8.8 shows a typical work-order backlog chart. Remember, if SMR is implemented correctly, most of the equipment would be monitored on a routine basis or continuously. In many cases, there would be redundancies that would reduce downtime and emergency work-orders. Therefore, the work-order backlog should decrease. As I have discussed before, the purpose of SMR is to eliminate unnecessary PMs that have no value—this also holds true for work-orders. The goal should be to decrease the backlog to one week maximum.

Maintenance Labor and Material Cost

Once the simplified maintenance reliability is implemented, you should see a gradual decrease in material cost. At the beginning, the cost will increase because we are implementing the action items that we have developed; however, once these action items are implemented, the material cost should decrease. The reason is that in many cases, we are detecting the failures before they happen, and as the result, we would eliminate the secondary failures. In some cases, we would have to redesign the system to eliminate the failure. In addition, it is important to know how much is being spent on implementing SMR action items. Material cost should be reviewed once a week by everyone in the maintenance department. Figure 8.9 shows a typical material cost graph for a typical company.

Labor and Material cost

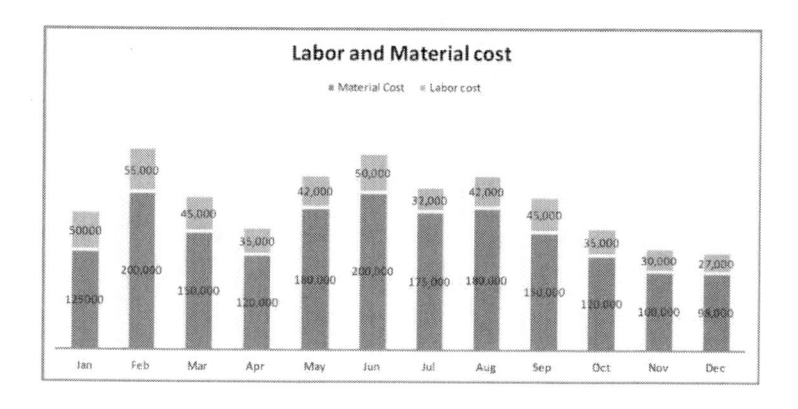

	Jan	Feb	Mar	Apr	May	Jun	Jul	Aug	Sep	Oct	Nov	Dec
Material Cost	125000	200,000	150,000	120,000	180,000	200,000	175,000	180,000	150,000	120,000	100,000	98,000
Labor cost	50000	55,000	45,000	35,000	42,000	50,000	32,000	42,000	45,000	35,000	30,000	27,000

Figure 8.9. Labor and material cost

Other Indicators

There are many other measurements that need to be developed to measure success. I just touched on some of the important ones; however, we should pay a close attention to: number or work-orders completed per day, number of work-orders completed per craft, and percentage of PMs completed on time.

Chapter Nine

Spare Parts

Having the correct number of spare parts is one of the keys to any successful maintenance program. It does not matter what kind of program you have developed in your organization—TPM, SMR, or any other program—you must identify all the critical spare parts, and either have them on your shelves in your maintenance store, or store them with a trusted vendor so spares can be easily obtained.

One of the great benefits of the SMR is that SMR-FMEA identifies which parts we need to have on the shelves. No other program can accomplish this.

Ask yourself how many times you have found a problem with component either through a PM or PDM and did not have the correct spare part. In addition, by the time the part arrived, the failure had already occurred, or you had to do some kind of temporary repair that was not adequate. Once the spare part arrived, you had to shut down the equipment and install the new part. You might not realize this, but by doing the job twice, the repair cost probably doubled, and operation suffered two major downtimes.

Today many parts manufacturers have reduced their stock, and they produce parts only when they are ordered. For example, if you need a hydraulic cylinder, it would take six to eight weeks to receive the cylinder unless you are willing to incur a high expedited cost. Sometimes even with expediting the part, it would still take a week to receive it. In addition, many parts are shipped from other countries, which will delay the timely replacement.

Spare Parts Strategy

As discussed in Chapter 3, we have two major types of failures: random and age-related. In the SMR-FMEA, we would assign an occurrence for both failures. You should use the occurrence number in the new RPN after the action is taken, as the number that is the approximate rate of failure.

Let's assume that the occurrence is 5, meaning the part fails approximately every three months. Therefore, your first safe assumption would be to have three parts on the shelf. The answer is correct if you could receive the part within three months. However, if the part takes eighteen months to manufacture, having three parts in stock would not be enough.

In addition, what is the part reliability confidence (RC)? For example, I have changed an electronic card two or three times before I could find the one that would actually work. Reliability confidence is a percentage of how confident we are that the spare part would work, and it is measured in percentage. In all cases, our goal through SMR is to find a more reliable part to replace the unreliable component; however, in some cases this is not possible because there are no other manufacturers, or the part is custom-made. Since there are no written publications, we must assume certain RC percent for each part. We should use our experience and history to develop such a number. As a rule of thumb, I use 90 percent (0.9) for random failures and 100 percent, or 1, for age-related failure. Figure 9.1 is a general calculation for the inventory levels for a single part.

$$N = \frac{L}{R \times RC\%} \times 100$$

Figure 9.1. Calculation for inventory levels

N = quantity of a single part

Lead Time = L

Rate of failure = F

Example: Lead-time is eighteen months, rate of failure is every three months, and we are 100 percent confident that the replacement would work.

N = 18/3 = 6 parts should be inventoried.

As mentioned in Chapter 3, there are four types of failures: age-associated gradual, age-associated sudden, random gradual, and random sudden. Figure 9.1 works for all four types of failures; however, it must be better defined for each type of failure. Let us assume that the guiderail on an indexing machine needs to be replaced every two years, and as we all know, this is an age-associated gradual failure. In addition, the lead time for these parts is twelve months. Using Figure 9.2, we can calculate the number of guiderails we would need to have on hand.

$$N = \frac{L}{R \times RC\%} \times 100$$

Figure 9.2. Calculation for number of guiderails needed

N = 12 month/ 24 month = .5

Since .5 is not a whole number, the question becomes how many parts we should have in inventory. Some might say we should round it to 1 and have one in stock. However, this is not the right answer. The answer would be zero. Since we would not need the part for two years, if it were ordered now, it would stay in our inventory for one extra year. The part should be ordered approximately one year before the failure. Most inventory management systems have a minimum ordering point. It notifies the department when it is time to purchase the part that has reached the minimum stock. In the above example, the inventory management system will order the above guiderail immediately. Therefore, there must be a different method to ensure that the guiderail is not ordered too early. There are three ways to do this: manually change the ordering date in the inventory system once the part is taken out, make work-order in the maintenance management system that would notify you at the time of order, or have a contract with a vendor to carry it in their inventory.

If this failure were a random failure, we would order one immediately. Random failures have no patterns and the time between the failures is not enough to make a sound decision. As a rule of thumb, for random failures, if N is equal or greater than .5, make sure you have one spare in stock. Remember what we have discussed here; only apply to the equipment that had original RPNs over 50.

Spare Parts Inventory Levels

In Chapter 8, we discussed the estimated replacement value. We also determined that normally the total maintenance cost should be 3.5 percent. However, this number includes material and the labor cost. Normally, the inventory level of the stock room should be the ERV multiplied by 3.5 percent, minus the labor. Then the result should be multiplied by 25 percent. Twenty percent is the high turnover inventory items, and 5 percent is the slow turnover critical parts that are custom made or have long lead-times. Let's look at an example.

EVR = 50 million dollars

Annual labor cost = 750, 000 dollars

(50 million x 3.5)/100= 1.75 million dollars

1.75 million - 750 thousand = 1 million

1 million x 25 percent= 250 thousand dollars

In the above example, the stockroom inventory value should be at minimum $250,000, $200,000 in fast and $50,000 in slow turnover items. Remember, the above is only a guideline. Some companies might choose to carry more inventory of spare parts than others, and that is perfectly fine; however, carrying less inventory than the calculated value could result in unnecessary downtime due to not having the correct parts on hand.

Today, many vendors will carry some or the entire required inventory. This will help the company in terms of cash flow. In addition, they can carry a higher amount of inventory than your company is willing to do. You would need to work with the purchasing department to implement such a program.

Chapter Ten

New Equipment and Reliability

Do you write your own specifications when purchasing new equipment? Does your specification include a section about reliability? I do not mean machine speed and general uptime requirement—I am implying to actual reliability study by the manufacturer.

The fact is reliability of the equipment should start in the initial design of the equipment; however, this is far from the truth. The majority of manufacturers do not even have a reliability engineer in their staff. This is not the same as the quality engineer. The quality department is responsible to make sure that the correct parts are ordered and installed on the equipment, and ensures quality workmanship; however, they have no idea how long a component, such as a flow control or a limit switch, might function properly.

Maintenance Manuals and Service Schedules

Maintenance manuals include drawings, part numbers, critical spare parts, component specifications such as limit switches pressure gauges, and level controls. At the end of the manual, you would normally find the service and preventative maintenance that is written for the equipment by the manufacturer. I'm not talking about small equipment such as a stand grinder or a small hoist—I'm talking about the large investments, such as molding machines, shot blasters, furnaces, and so on.

By right, the purchaser quickly purchases all the critical parts to make sure they are on hand in case they are needed. Some parts are normally used within the first few months or years; however, others sit on the shelf until they are obsolete, and they are never replaced.

The manufacturer's suggested service and preventative maintenance is a good start; however, it is not enough for ensuring the reliability of the equipment. Usually these manuals are developed based on experience and some historical information from the vendors and customers. Remember, the manufacturer of the equipment does not operate the equipment every day; they might only operate it for a short period of time, which is called a trial run. Some manufacturers do not even have this capability, and they would never see the machine operate until it is installed by the customer.

Once the new equipment is installed and running for a while, the reliability issues start appearing. Normally during the warranty period, the manufacturer will replace defective parts; however, the reliability of the equipment will not increase. This is particularly true with a custom-made machine.

Few times, the equipment has design flaws that are addressed by the original manufacturer during the warranty period. However, these fixes may or may not increase the reliability of the equipment.

Eventually, if the reliability issues are not addressed, the performance and the availability will decrease. As the result, the productivity of the equipment would diminish. For example, a hydraulic press is designed for a hundred cycles per hour, but we might have to decrease the speed to ninety-five cycles, because at the designed speed the upper ram packing leaks oil and causes a quality issue. In many cases, these types of performance issues would not get resolved and the company (purchaser) ends up accepting the diminished performance. Look around in your plant and find out how many equipment you will find that have not performed to the designed criteria since they were installed.

Writing Specifications for Reliability

To ensure that manufacturer would evaluate the reliability issues with the equipment, we should include a reliability section in our initial equipment specification. Writing a complete equipment specification is beyond the scope of this book. For now, I am going to provide you with the necessary elements that need to be in your specification.

First thing you must remember: The manufacturer's first and most concern is functionality and profitability, not reliability. The sooner the equipment is designed and functions, the sooner the manufacturer can receive the last payment and move on to the next project. This is especially true when the equipment is large and custom-made. Normally, you the customer must educate them of your reliability requirements. In your specifications, you should write before the proposal is submitted, the manufacturer ABC will set up a meeting with the purchaser XYZ to review, and understand XYZ's reliability requirements that shall be included as a part of this proposal.

In this meeting, you should take the manufacturer through what you have learned in this book. Provide them with a copy of the SMR-FMEA. Make sure they understand that they have to develop the correct maintenance programs based on the result of the SMR-FMEA.

Once the equipment is ordered, you should hold routine meetings to make sure that the manufacturer is making progress on developing the SMR-FMEA. Review the RPN numbers and make sure they are correct. Make certain that the high RPNs have the correct maintenance options and action items. In addition, these action items are being implemented into the design. Where action items are mainly developing PMs, make sure that the manufacturer is providing you with them.

There is a Cost

If you are purchasing a locomotive from a major manufacturer, most of what I have explained in this chapter is already completed by the seller; however, if you are purchasing a custom-made injection molding machine, most likely no one has ever formally reviewed the reliability of the equipment. Adding a reliability section to your specification will increase the price of the machine; however, some or all of the additional cost can be negotiated. The most important fact is, the price increase will pay for itself in the first few months of operation. Remember the saying you get what you pay for.

Having a section about reliability in your specification forces the manufacturer to review all the subcomponents and their lifecycle. In some cases, they might choose more reliable or redundant parts. In addition, it makes the manufacturer more knowledgeable about the subcomponents; therefore, they may create better PMs in the equipment manuals.

The most important benefits are that you would know what to expect about the reliability of the equipment and that you have a documented SMR-FMEA that was developed by the manufacturer that shows they have reduced the resultant RPNs. If the equipment does not hold true to those RPNs, you can always demand further actions. For example, this document can be very valuable if the equipment is purchased for $5,000,000, and does not meet the expected reliability criteria.

What is Critical?

Before you start writing any type of specification, you must fully determine the critical elements.

Critical to safety (CTS)

The first and the most important one is critical to safety (CTS). This would be all the designed characteristics that would make the equipment safe and also meets or exceeds OSHA, state, and local regulations, such as handrails, steps, pinch points, lockout tag-out, etc....

Most manufactures have a disclaimer in their operating manuals, stating that before performing any work, equipment must be in zero mechanical and electrical state. This is a dangerous statement, because it puts all the responsibility of the lock-out tag-out procedures on the end user, and I always disagree with it. Suppose the manufacturer did not provide the means to drain the hydraulic accumulator in a press, and you have written a lock-out tag-out procedure that turned off the hydraulics and the electrical system, but it did not address the accumulator. In this case, the equipment still possesses potential energy, which is the accumulator. Since the manufacturer has a disclaimer in their operating manual, all the liability could fall on your company. As a part of the CTS, make sure you always have the manufacturer write the initial lock-out tag-out. If you modify it, make sure you have the manufacturer is in agreement with the change.

Critical to environmental (CTE)

What are the equipment emissions? Are these emissions harmful to the environment, or employees? These are some of the questions that are critical to the environmental department. In some cases, you might have to purchase additional emission control systems; in other cases, these controls are part of the purchase package. In both cases, the manufacturer must provide the seller with the correct information about the potential quantity of emissions, emission points, and type of emissions. The manufacturer must also meet or exceed all the federal, state, and local laws in regards to the environmental controls equipment.

Critical to quality (CTQ)

CTQ is defined as what is critical to the quality of the product that is produce by the purchased equipment. Normally this area is defined by the quality department and ultimately by the customer. Critical to quality could be dimensions, shape, chemical or physical properties. The specification should have well defined parameters for the items that are critical to quality. These parameters should be monitored by the purchaser or the manufacturer even after the equipment is installed and running. Since the CTQ is timeless, the manufacturer has a greater responsibility, and must submit quantified measurements that indicate quality parameters that are in control. The manufacturer shall submit a plan to purchaser to ensure that all the CTQs have been addressed.

Sometimes, it is not necessary to include CTQ in the specifications. For example, if you are purchasing a dust collector, it might not have any effect to the quality of the product that you are producing in your plant.

Critical to operations (CTO)

Normally what is important to the operation is the production rate, including performance, ease of operation, and quality. The quality part is defined in the CTQ section. The specification should clearly define the operations expectation. For example, the molding machine shall produce an average of 245 molds per hour. In this example, I mentioned "average," meaning the speed of the machine must be higher to meet this specification. Many times, purchasers make the mistake of putting a rate or a speed in the specification without emphasizing the speed is the average rate. This is important, because if the top speed of the machine were 245 molds per hour, on average it would never perform at that rate.

Let's assume that Figure 10.1 represents the speed of molding machine's normal distribution with a top speed of 245 molds per hour. If the standard deviation of the speed is five molds per hour, the average speed would be 230 molds per hour.

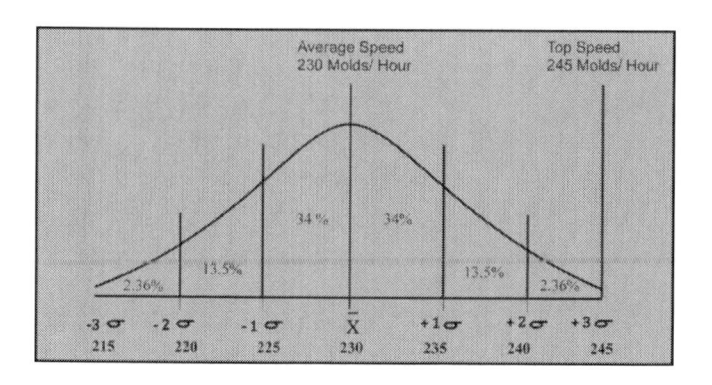

Figure 10.1. Normal distribution for 230 molds per hour molding machine

Figure 10.2 represents the normal distribution for a molding machine with an average speed of 245 molds per hour. If our goal is to produce 245 molds per hour on an average, based on the same standard deviation of five molds per hour, our top speed should be 260 molds per hour.

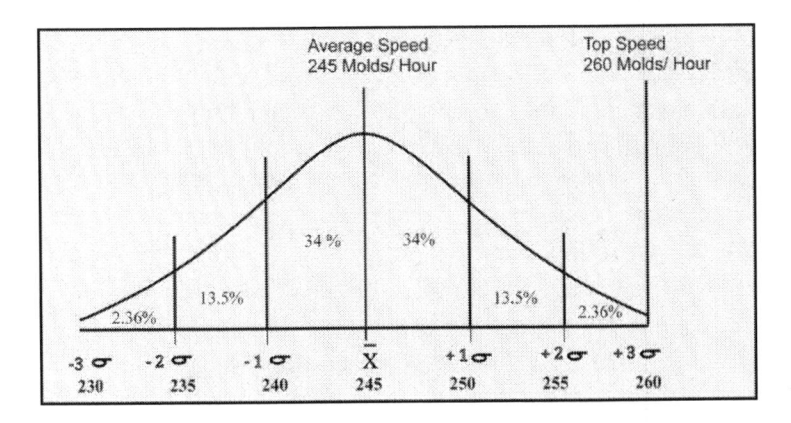

Figure 10.2. Normal distribution for 245 molds per hour molding machine

Critical to maintenance (CTM)

This signifies the ease of maintaining the equipment, meaning being able to find the components and have adequate access to work on them. People who have worked on compact cars truly understand this. Knowing which components have higher chances of failure, well-defined diagnostics, correct maintenance and repair manuals, well-defined preventative maintenance, and correct spare parts are all critical to the maintenance department. In addition, it is critical to have the correct final drawings, mechanical, electrical, controls, and process. These documents should be received and reviewed by the purchaser, in this case meaning the maintenance can easily interpret the drawings and manuals. Remember, do not approve the final design. The final design is the manufacturer's responsibility.

Critical to reliability (CTR)

Identification of the random and age-related failures, knowing what parts need to be replaced frequently and the frequency, knowing what components can be monitored continuously for vibration temperature, or any other type of conditional maintenance, are critical to reliability of the equipment. In addition, it is important to know the useful life of the major age-related components. For example, let's look at a rotary type air compressor. Air compressors consist of a few major components: air-end, motor, heat exchangers for oil and air, air and oil pressure and temperature switches, oil reservoir, main starter, and controls. One must ask the manufacturer if there is a history of failures on any of the above components, or if the manufacturer has ever done an FMEA on the major components. In few cases, the manufacturer already possesses this information and is willing to share it with the buyer; however, most of the time this material is not available. If there is no information available, at minimum, we should identify the random failures that could occur frequently; for example, pressure switches, and ask the manufacturer for redundancies or get suppliers permission to install our own. We can also complete a full SMR-FMEA on the major components, knowing we do not have enough information on the occurrence. However, we would use the manufacturer's input, or make an educated assumption based on experience. The goal is to make the equipment 100 percent reliable. Whatever we can do at the beginning of the project will help us in the long run to achieve our goal. Remember, after the warranty period is over, you are on your own.

Other Benefits of Simplified Maintenance Reliability

1- Eliminates PMs that have no value

When a SMR-FMEA is completed, all the recommended actions are generated based on the RPNs and the type of failures. Therefore, many of the older PMs have to be either disregarded or modified. Remember, as we discussed in Chapter 8, the goal should be to drive the maintenance program to 40 percent conditional maintenance. Therefore, many of the traditional PMs can be eliminated.

2- Improves productivity

As you implement SMR throughout the plant, uptime should start improving, which will have a direct positive effect on productivity. Of course, this does not happen overnight. Most of the recommended actions from the SMR-FMEA must be implemented before you realize any improvement in productivity and availability. This is why it is so important to measure the OEE and reevaluate the recommended actions from the SMR-FMEA.

3- Reduces emergency work-orders

Once the program is implemented, the reliability of the equipment should increase, as the result emergency breakdowns would decrease. Obviously, less breakdowns will result in less emergency work-orders. It is a good practice to chart the number of emergency work-orders produced each month. Use this chart as one of the indicators to measure the success.

4- Reduces maintenance overtime hours

As we all know, most emergency work-orders require overtime because they take away time from the scheduled maintenance work. As I discussed before, with successful implementation of SMR, the number of emergency work-orders generated would be decreased.

5- Reduces annual shutdown duration and cost

Most companies have one or two weeks of shutdown to install capital equipment, or perform maintenance tasks on major equipment that the PMs are behind, or cannot be completed within a reasonable time during the operating hours. The problem is; however, that many times, work is performed on a subcomponents that have random failures—for example, changing proximity switches, light bulbs in pilot lights, replacing coils in starters. Annual shutdowns should only be designed for capital or major maintenance projects that are categorized as age-related.

Once you implement SMR, all equipment should be categorized into one of the categories in Chapter 6; this would identify all the correct equipment that need to be worked on during the annual shutdown. As a result, not only the duration of the shutdown but also the cost of shutdown would decrease.

6- Improves maintenance planning

When the program is implemented, SMR-FMEA will include all the actions that need to be taken for each equipment and component. Some components would be continuously monitored; others would require time-based maintenance. In any case, since planners, maintenance supervisors, and operation personnel are aware of the types of maintenance that need to be performed, this would make the planning and scheduling more efficient. There would be no communication gap between the operation and maintenance. All employees would know the severity, consequence, and the occurrence of the failures, and the actions that need to be taken.

7- *Identifies training requirements for maintenance and operations*

In many cases, on the SMR-FMEA, the cause of the problem is identified to be lack of improper training, or an incorrect operating procedure. For example, in Exercise 1, it was determined that proper training was needed for installation of sheaves and V-belts.

8- *Truly identifies operations and maintenance responsibilities*

As I mentioned at the beginning of this book, SMR is not just a maintenance program. This becomes evident once you complete one or two projects. Some of the recommended actions would be maintenance, and others would be operation's responsibility. For example, in Exercise 1, we decided to install continuous vibration monitoring. The signal from the vibration monitoring could be sent to the control room, where operation can easily monitor and notify the maintenance personnel if vibration is above the normal limits. In this case, monitoring and notification is performed by operation, and corrective action is taken by the maintenance department.

9- *Reduces total maintenance cost*

I already discussed that the program should reduce excessive overtime, but that is not all. Reliable equipment equates to fewer failures, and fewer failures requires less replacements and less cost. Early detection of the initial failure and making the necessary correction is the key to reducing maintenance cost. For example, in Exercise 1, let's assume that the bearing monitoring system has alarmed us that the bearing is showing low-level vibration. Initially this problem could be result of minor misalignment or lack of lube; however, if the issue is not addressed soon, it could cause major bearing or shaft failure. These failures could also cause a major downtime that is not acceptable by production.

10- Identifies design issues that must be addressed

It is important to understand that if the SMR-FMEA shows that the occurrence is 9 or 10, and the severity is 7 or higher, this is no longer a maintenance issue, it is a design issue. For example, in Exercise 1, let's assume that we have to replace the V-belts every two days because they break, and this failure causes downtime. We also know that the V-belts are installed properly. This is no longer a maintenance issue. It could be that the V-belts were not sized properly during the original design, and replacing them every two days has become an accepted practice.

SMR also identifies the true capital projects that need to be completed to reduce failures. Normally these projects can easily be identified with the SMR-FMEA. These are projected with high occurrence and severity numbers that maintenance programs have had little success in reducing the failures. It is always easier to justify these projects by ensuring that you are able to show the severity, occurrence, and the history of the failures.

Final Words

Every time I complete a seminar on SMR, some people are skeptical about implementation and the success of this program. These people normally say, "We are busy, and do not have the time to implement the simplified maintenance reliability in our plant."

I always ask them if they have a better program to offer. The whole reason you have been reading this book is that your company has equipment reliability issues—and probably has had them for some time. Most of the time, people do not have the time to implement this program, because they are always putting out fires and working on emergencies. Unless you implement simplified maintenance reliability, your struggles in your company will continue

The facts are, I have implemented simplified maintenance reliability in several companies and currently have become a way of life in these companies. Frankly, the program is very easy and can be simplified in four simple steps.

1. Use the 4-Q rule, and choose the first project.

2. Apply SMR-FMEA principles; choose the correct type of failures and maintenance options.

3. Come up with counter-measures and apply them.

4. Monitor the results and fine-tune them.

Remember this: You are not alone. Many companies are struggling with equipment downtime and failures. As I mentioned before, I have also experienced the same issues; however, I am confident once you start using the methods described in this book, you will start seeing the benefits quickly.

Appendix

SMR Component Charts

Maintenance Option Chart

	Sudden (S)	Gradual (G)
Age Associated (A)	Time Based Replacement. (TR) Redundant systems. Frequent variation monitoring. (VM) Training (T)	Time Based maintenance. (TM) Time based replacement. (TR) Event based maintenance. (EB) Training. (T)
Random (R)	Run to failure. (RF) Redundant systems. reengineering alternatives. (RA) Frequent variation monitoring. (VM). Training.(T).	Event based maintenance. (EB) Redundant systems. Training. (T). Frequent variation monitoring. (VM)

Severity

Severity	Ranking	Criteria
Very High	9-10	Failure affects safety or involves the noncompliance to government regulations. May endanger machine assembly operator (9 with warning, 10 without warning)
High	7-8	High degree of operations dissatisfaction due to nature of the failure, such as serious disruption to process, high degree of rework and downtime
Moderate	4-5-6	Failure causes some operations dissatisfaction which may include performance deterioration, this may result in unscheduled rework/ repairs and or damage to the equipment
Low	2-3	Due to the nature of the failure operations experiences slight deterioration in performance or process.
Very Low	1	Failure would not cause any noticeable effect to operation performance, process. Operations would not be affected by this failure.

Occurrence

Ranking	Description
10	≥ 1 occurrence per shift
9	≥ 1 occurrence per day
8	≥ 1 per week
7	≥ 1 per 2 to 3 weeks
6	≥ 1 per month
5	≥ 1 per quarter
4	≥ 1 per 6 months
3	≥ 1 per year
2	≥ 1 per 2 years
1	< 1 per 3 years

Detection

Detection	Ranking	Detection Criteria
None	10	Controls will not or can not detect the existence of the initial failure mode. No known controls are available to detect failure mode
Very Low	9	Controls probably will not detect the existence of initial failure mode.
Low	7-8	Controls have a poor chance of detecting the existence of initial failure mode.
Moderate	5-6	Controls may detect the existence of the initial failure mode
High	3-4	Controls have a good chance of detecting the initial mode. Process automatically detects failure modes.
Very High	1-2	Current controls almost certain to detect the failure mode. Reliable detection controls are known with similar processes. Process automatically detects initial failure.

Action Items, **88**
Availability, **93**, **95**, **98**
Average, 103
baghouse, **74**
calculation, **100**, **108**
chances, **119**
components, **74**, **83**, **87**, **91**, **99**, **119**, **120**, **122**
conditional maintenance, **88**, **91**, **120**, **121**
consequence, **122**
correct maintenance option, **91**, **114**
Critical to Environmental, **116**
Critical to Maintenance, **119**
Critical to Operations, **117**
Critical to Quality, **117**
Critical to safety, **116**
CTE, **116**
CTM, **119**
CTO, **117**
CTQ, **117**
CTR, **120**
CTS, **116**
detection, **72**, **73**, **74**, **76**, **77**, **79**, **80**, **81**, **82**, **83**, **92**, **96**, **98**, **123**
Detection, **77**
distribution, **118**, **119**
downtime, **74**, 78, **93**, 94, 96, 97, 98, 100, 102, 105, 111, 123, 124
Element, **75**, **76**
equipment, **57**, 78, **83**, **85**, **87**, **91**, **93**, **94**, 96, **100**, **101**, **105**, **107**, **110**, **112**, **113**, **114**, **115**, **116**, **117**, **119**, **120**, **121**, **122**, **123**, **124**
ERV, **99**, **100**, **101**, **110**
Estimated Replacement Value, **99**
examine, **79**
example, **44**, **72**, **73**, **74**, **75**, **76**, **77**, **78**, **79**, **80**, **82**, **89**, **90**, **93**, **94**, **95**, 97, 100, 102, 103, 107, 108, 110, 111, 113, 115, 117, 120, 122, 123, 124
facilitator, **85**, **87**
Facilitator, **85**
FMEA, **74**, **75**, **76**, **77**, **79**, **80**, **82**, **83**, **86**, **87**, **88**, **89**, **91**, **98**, **99**, **108**, **114**, **115**, **120**, **121**, **122**, **123**, **124**, **125**
Gradual, **44**, **75**, **109**
Hidden failure, 89
Hidden Failures, **89**
Implementing, **85**
indicator, 103
initial failure, **72**, **73**, **79**, **82**
inventory levels, **110**
maintenance department, **100**, **101**, **102**, **105**, **123**
Maintenance Manuals, **112**
maintenance options, **44**, **79**, **125**
maintenance programs, **124**
manufacturer, **112**, **113**, **114**, **115**, **116**, **117**, **119**, **120**
mathematical, **94**
metrics, **93**
molding machine, **72**, **115**, **117**, **118**, **119**
occurrence, **73**, **74**, **76**, **77**, **79**, **80**, **81**, **82**, **83**, **92**, **96**, **98**, **108**, **120**, **122**, **124**
OEE, **93**, **95**, **96**, **97**, **98**, **121**
Overall Equipment Effectiveness, **93**, **95**
performance, **57**, **94**, **95**, **96**, **97**, **113**, **117**
PMs, 87, 102, 105, 106, 114, 115, 120, 122
process, **74**, **85**, **87**, **119**
productivity, **113**, **121**

Random, **109**, **110**
ranking, 72, 73, 80
Redundant, **44**
reliability, **73**, **82**, **88**, **103**, **105**, **108**, **112**, **113**, **114**, **115**, **120**, **121**, **124**, **125**
RPN, **73**, **74**, **76**, **77**, **79**, **80**, **82**, **83**, **87**, **91**, **98**, **108**, **114**
safety checks, 86, 87
severity, **73**, **74**, **76**, **79**, **80**, **81**, **82**, **83**, **92**, **98**, **122**, **124**
simplified maintenance reliability, **125**
six-sigma, **99**
SMR, **74**, **75**, **76**, **77**, **79**, **80**, **82**, **83**, **85**, **86**, **87**, **88**, **89**, **91**, **96**, **98**, **99**, **101**, **103**, **105**, **107**, **108**, **114**, **115**, **120**, **121**, **122**, **123**, **124**, **125**
SMR-FMEA, **76**, **87**, **88**, **98**, **107**, **114**, **121**, **124**
Spare Parts, **107**
Spare parts strategy, **108**
Specifications, **114**
sudden, **44**, **75**, **79**, **80**, **82**, **91**, **109**
TPM, **107**
traditional, **76**, **121**
Types of Work-Orders, **102**
variation, **44**
Vibration, **42**
Work-Order, **103**
Work-Order Backlog, **103**

Made in the USA
Lexington, KY
25 June 2016